DATE DUE

GAYLORD			PRINTED IN U.S.A.

Books by James F. Fixx

Games for the Superintelligent (1972)
More Games for the Superintelligent (1976)
The Complete Book of Running (1977)
Solve It! (1978)
*The Complete Runner's Day-by-Day Log and
    Calendar* (annually since 1979)
Jim Fixx's Second Book of Running (1980)
Jackpot! (1982)

JACKPOT!

JACKPOT!
by James F. Fixx

RANDOM HOUSE 🏠 *NEW YORK*

Library of Congress Cataloging in Publication Data

Fixx, James F.
　　Jackpot!

　　　1. Fixx, James F.　2. Runners (Sports)—
United States—Biography.　3. Sportswriters—
United States—Biography. I. Title.
√ GV1061.15.F59A34　　796.4′26　[B]　81–15747
ISBN 0–394–50899–8　　　　　　　AACR2

Manufactured in the United States of America
24689753
First Edition

For Alice,
who for better
or for worse
saw it all
happen

Read through this book, and ye will find in it the greatest and most marvelous characteristics of the people especially of Armenia, Persia, India, and Tartary, as they are severally related in the present work by Marco Polo . . . , who states distinctly what things he saw and what things he heard from others. For this book will be a truthful one. . . . Wishing in his secret thoughts that the things he had seen and heard should be made public by the present work, for the benefit of those who could not see them with their own eyes, he himself . . . caused the things which are contained in the present work to be written.

—*The Travels of Marco Polo*

I believe that this is a very great continent, until today unknown. . . . If this be a continent, it is a marvelous thing.

—Columbus, *Journal*

Contents

I

"The Fates Were Exceedingly Kind"

Manhattan.

Morning.

A crisply functional suite of offices in a glass-and-steel building of Euclidean symmetry.

Four men and a woman sit at an oval conference table of teak that has been fragrantly oiled. Pencils, their points newly sharpened, and lined writing tablets have been arranged in front of each.

Three of the people at the table are lawyers: Arnold Zephyr, the firm's founder, whose services command $200 an hour; Archibald Hellas, an assistant, $100 an hour; and Sam Binder III, who has only recently been anointed by the Harvard Law School, $60 an hour. My wife, Alice, and I are the other two. The Zephyr firm, which specializes in representing men and women in show business and the popular arts, has been recommended as a reliable source of advice about what to do with the considerable sum of money my recent book, *The Complete Book of Running,* has earned. Two or three weeks earlier Alice and I had an exploratory meeting with the three lawyers. The purpose of the present gathering is to hear the distilled essence of their thoughts.

Zephyr, who has a lean, well-bred look and numbers among his close friends several people who write regularly for *Foreign Affairs,* speaks first.

"We have three extremely interesting proposals," he says. "All of them can save you a good deal of money in taxes."

He turns to Hellas, whose necktie, I notice, is flecked with a pattern of embroidered tennis racquets.

"Arch," he says, "why don't you explain our thinking?"

Hellas opens a manila folder and, turning to Alice and me, asks, "Are you familiar with hopper cars?"

He explains that hopper cars, or as they are sometimes called, gondola cars, cost about $45,000 each. The investor buys one or more (or, if he is in straitened circumstances, part of a car), leases it or them to a railroad that is short of such rolling stock, and in return receives financial benefits known as investment tax credits and depreciation write-offs.

"There's just one minor problem," Hellas continues. "If the economy should slow down you could very easily find yourself with hopper cars for which there was, at least temporarily, little demand."

Binder speaks. "You certainly wouldn't want that to happen," he says. He looks worried.

"That's the last thing Jim and Alice would want," Zephyr says. "Maybe this would be the time to move along to computers."

Hellas opens a second folder. "This is something you're going to find fascinating," he tells us. He is smiling.

Hellas explains that he and his colleagues want to recommend that we buy some computers, lease them to corporations in need of such instruments and then, when they have become obsolete, sell them in South America or some other region where computing requirements are not as rigorous as they are in our own country.

"You'd be surprised," he explains, "what a good market there is for computers that by our standards are no longer very useful."

"What happens," I ask, "if for some reason a buyer can't be found for the obsolete computers?"

Furrows crease the brows of the three men. Zephyr says, "You've put your finger on one of the main problems with computers."

Binder adds, "And it can be quite a serious problem, too."

"There is, however, a third idea," Zephyr goes on. "This one, I'm happy to say, doesn't have any of the disadvantages of either hopper cars or computers."

Hellas opens another folder. "Are you aware of slums?" he asks.

The investor, he explains, buys a run-down apartment building, pays to have it gutted and restored, and in return receives attractive tax advantages.

Zephyr, nodding, says to me, "We definitely see you and Alice in slums."

The meeting ends. Alice and I promise the lawyers to give consideration to their recommendations. Then we leave. I am, I find, more befuddled about what to do with the money than I was before I received their advice.

Nor, during this period, were all my confusions, or for that matter all my mistakes, monetary. One evening, in a packed auditorium, I delivered the most artful speech I had ever given. I had notes with me but, buoyed up by my unwonted eloquence, had no need to refer to them. Each idea, moved along by deftly turned transitions, flowed seamlessly into the next; anecdotes not only received appreciative laughter but illustrated, precisely and cogently, the points I sought to make. Afterward there was much applause and I spent an hour signing autographs.

It was only later that an irreverent friend pointed out that during my entire virtuoso performance the fly of my trousers had been quite noticeably unzipped.

Both incidents are paradigms of the sorts of experiences I have been having ever since, in 1977, I wrote a book that for nearly two years lingered at the top of the major best-seller lists and in the process took me, a thoroughly unexceptional person, to places and introduced me to people whose existence I had until then scarcely imagined. The present book is a reconnaissance report based on the adventures I had. Throughout most of it my vantage point is that unfailingly fascinating but, for obvious reasons, only infrequently visited outpost of our culture where money, renown and the American dream coalesce.

At one time I thought of calling this book simply *Spy*. That title seemed to me accurately indicative of what I felt I had been up to. I was in effect an undercover agent, spending my days where I really had no business being. For even though in the past three or four years my writing has earned me a good deal of money and enough attention to satisfy all but the most irredeemably greedy of egomaniacs, in many ways I feel entirely unchanged by what has happened. Like Marco Polo, who, despite a quarter-century of wandering through the oddities and enigmas of thirteenth-century Asia, retained the practical, level-headed perceptions of a workaday Venetian, I am still quite recognizably myself. No matter how unfamiliar some parts of my world may have become, my intellectual and emotional compass has not, so far as I can tell, been deflected any more significantly than Marco Polo's was. (Having looked over an early draft of this chapter during a vacation from college, my son John wrote me the following note: "Your experience, perhaps, has been more like Columbus's than Marco Polo's. Columbus wasn't trying to discover America any more than you were trying to write a best seller, make lots of money, etc. Marco Polo *set out* to discover; Columbus simply stumbled on something he couldn't possibly comprehend at that moment." The distinction John made seems to me a precise and telling one.)

My resistance to temperamental alterations is no doubt partly a matter of nothing more obscure or complicated than age. When my book appeared I was already in my forties, so I'd had plenty of opportunity to learn what was important to me and what wasn't. I knew how I wanted to live and how I didn't and what changes in my life I was willing and unwilling to make. In reviewing two books about Gary Cooper for the *New York Times,* Anatole Broyard remarked that Cooper conveyed "a sense of a rather ordinary man enjoying himself." That seems to me a fair description of what has happened to me. I've enjoyed myself a lot, much of the time anyway. And Lord knows I feel ordinary enough. Over the past few years, in fact, I have often experienced a sense of wonderment about exactly what it means to have more money than God probably ever intended writers to have, and to be more widely known than most people, unless they are talk-show hosts or mass murderers, ever become.

There is also another reason that my vivid sense of the curiosities and absurdities of fame has remained more or less uncontaminated. It is that I had previously been so thoroughly insulated from renown that I had managed to remain mostly unsmudged by its effluents. For one thing, I had never taken more than a distant interest in celebrities, supposing them to be, for the most part, creatures of their press agents' imaginations, or in advanced cases their own, and therefore no more fit for sustained notice than so many puffs of smoke. I knew, of course, that for many people the lives of their more radiant brethren have a mesmerizing fascination. But I also remembered Daniel Boorstin's ironical definition of *celebrity:* "being well known for being well known." A few years ago a perceptive friend, Susan Margolis, wrote a book, *Fame,* in which she tried to put her finger on the enduring fascination celebrities have for us. Even though she had been a lifetime student of the subject, and was an uncommonly discerning one, I could not at the time imagine how she had contrived to keep her mind on her topic for as long as she plainly had. Fame just wasn't a phenomenon that attracted or interested me.

I was not, on the other hand, totally unacquainted with it, at least at a safe remove. Over the years, as a journalist, I had met a number of men and not a few women whose fame was both indisputable and incandescent—Arnold Toynbee, Margaret Mead, Henry and Clare Boothe Luce and, among politicians, Lyndon Johnson, Hubert Humphrey and Richard Nixon. Their glitter seemed remote and mostly irrelevant, however, for whatever voltage I possessed, even after my book's appearance, was much lower and more localized. True, over the years my by-line had appeared in some important magazines, and on three or four of them I had even held prominent editorial posts —articles editor, managing editor, executive editor and so forth. I had been interviewed on various radio programs and several television shows, and one year my name appeared in the *New Yorker*'s annual Christmas poem:

> . . . *Regards from all us wassailniks,*
> *To Elliott Burch and James F. Fixx.* . . .

Even in the small town in Connecticut where I lived, however, practically no one knew who I was. On a Saturday I could walk along the main street, wearing scuffed hiking boots and a sweater that was falling apart at the elbows, and most of my neighbors could not have told you whether I was a magazine editor or a plumber.

Within a matter of weeks my anonymity disappeared. Well-knownness, unfamiliar and occasionally baffling, lapped at me. I was referred to, not just once but repeatedly, as "world-famous." Pete Gogolak, a Connecticut neighbor who remains one of the top AFL-NFL scorers of all time, told me at a party, "You're Mr. Running." I was caricatured, along with Steve Cauthen, Sir Edmund Hillary and Fran Tarkenton, by Hirschfeld, the celebrity cartoonist, and interviewed by two university sociologists who to my astonishment accepted even my most trivial observations with grave seriousness. At a scientific conference in Manhattan I heard myself referred to simply as "Fixx"—no first name needed—and at another conference a distinguished psychiatrist asked me, "How does it feel to be a national figure?" *The Complete Book of Running* inspired a sermon by a rabbi in San

Diego, a song by a nightclub performer in Sydney, Australia, a poem by a poet in Houston, Texas. On a flight to the West Coast the pilot, having learned that I was aboard his aircraft, came back to my seat to talk about running, and men, women and children on six continents (Antarctica was the exception) wrote to solicit my autograph and picture. William F. Buckley mentioned me in the lead paragraph of one of his newspaper columns, a sports magazine listed me among "The People Who Run Running," and I was described in a television commercial (along with Tony Dorsett of the Dallas Cowboys, Jim Rice of the Boston Red Sox and the jockey Darrel McHargue) as one of "a whole new crop of heroes." The president of a major New England university said, "You're my idol," and Beningno S. Aquino, while a political prisoner at Fort Bonifacio in the Philippines, told a reporter for the *New York Times* that he had read *The Complete Book of Running* and had "become a devotee."

In addition to its quota of well-knownness, the book brought a number of discoveries as well. Not a few of these concerned money, which, when it appears in uncommon abundance, has a gravitational force as irresistible as that of any celestial black hole. Almost everyone within range moves in its direction, including a wonderfully inventive and variegated multitude of men and women with advice to offer. Within a few months after the publication of my book I had been importuned by a galaxy of lawyers, stockbrokers, financial advisors, agents, managers and a man who, as we shall see, proposed with complete seriousness to put my name and likeness on posters, T-shirts and the dials of wristwatches.

One of the first advisors to make an appearance was the owner of a financial planning firm in the Northeast. He wrote me a letter, on embossed stationery so luxuriantly crisp it may for all I know have been parchment, in which he said, "Our growth has been attributed to respect shown to the client's individual, personal matters and to his innermost feelings." He could hardly have known, poor fellow, that his prose style, in that sentence alone, had already committed considerable mayhem on my innermost feelings. Yet I remained hopeful that someone, either of his breed or of some other, would eventually come along to unsnarl the confusions in which I increasingly found myself enmeshed.

Before the book's appearance I had seldom had more than a few spare dollars at any one time. When I worked for *McCall's*, the company's president, Henry Bowes, in an effort to keep his executives content, arranged for free financial advice from a Manhattan accounting firm. One day I had a talk with one of the accountants Bowes had engaged. Seeing how little money I had, he shrugged politely and said, "I'm afraid there isn't much we can do for you." It was therefore with bewilderment that, a decade later, I found myself being asked to let my mind roam such *terrae incognitae* as tax shelters, municipal bond funds and the arcane mysteries of gondola cars, computers and slums.

My confusions gave rise to a hope that was not unrelated in spirit to Harold Ross's quixotic search for an editorial miracle worker who would finally, as one staff member put it, make everything at the *New Yorker* as "neat as a trivet or an apple-pie." For a long time I cherished the notion that sooner or later I would find someone who, in his or her benevolent wisdom, would tell me what to do when it came to just about everything. Under his kindly dictatorial tutelage I would discover where to invest my money for good yields and exemplary safety, which business proposals to accept and which to reject, and how to arrange my time in order to accomplish all the absorbing nonliterary tasks that now presented themselves, but nonetheless enjoy the solitary stretches I needed in order to get some writing done.

There was no shortage of candidates for the post. Having read a flippantly skeptical comment of mine about the financial efficacy of slum rehabilitation, an Albuquerque real estate developer wrote to say he could not agree more heartily. "Frankly," he told me, "I don't see you in slums at all. I see you in single-family homes in the best young, middle-class subdivisions of Albuquerque and Phoenix." A retired television executive in North Carolina offered me the services of his son, who, in the father's words, "takes on a new client only after exhaustive and comprehensive in-depth analysis." (He also ventured a somber warning: "I don't know if you would qualify.") A New York City stockbroker, having recommended that I put my money into futures contracts, sent me a brochure that included, tucked into the fine print, this unsettling observation: "These securities involve a high degree of risk and are suitable only for persons who can afford to lose their entire investment." At a book-and-author luncheon in Manhattan a young woman of steamily handsome good looks asked me to autograph her copy of *The Complete Book of Running*. As I handed it back to her she pressed a note into my palm. It read, "It is my hope that I can meet with you to discuss your investments." Finally, a Suffolk Downs horse dealer sent me a notice printed in Old English type adorned with serifs and nodes so sumptuously suggestive of aristocratic breeding as to be all but unreadable. It invited "queries about Thoroughbred racing and its unique investment opportunities."

Somehow none of these seemed quite right. I therefore kept looking, with results that will become manifest later in these pages.

The idea for this book began gnawing at me almost as soon as *The Complete Book of Running* crept tentatively onto the low rungs of the best-seller lists. There exists in America a vast, generally unnoticed apparatus whose sole functions are to serve celebrity and to feed on it. So long as you do not set yourself apart from your fellows, it remains dormant and is, in that quiescent state, almost entirely invisible. As an experiment, ask one of the chief lecture agencies—Harry Walker, Inc., say, or the Program Corporation of America—to take you on as a client. If your name is not widely known, no matter how spellbinding a public speaker you may be, nothing will happen. Receive a Cabinet appointment, however, or participate in a nicely publicized political burglary or write a best-selling book, and Harry Walker or PCA will track you down with offers of $2,500 (or two or three times that amount if they consider you *really* special) for an easy forty minutes' work. Once you have distinguished yourself, in short, the celebrity apparatus sets out to find you. Your telephone rings. Mail arrives by the bundle. Offers are made, deals proposed, opportunities described. People whose sincerity all but blinds you ask only the privilege of multiplying your money, enhancing your career and augmenting your fame.

In a society that numbers among its journalistic ornaments such magazines as *People* and *Us,* not to mention uncountable gossip columns, no one can long remain in innocence about the manifestations of renown. It is, on the other hand, vouchsafed to few of us to witness the celebrity apparatus from within. This, once its tireless machinery had me in its soothing embrace, became my fascinating privilege.

It is not, however, proximity alone that prompts me to record my experiences. Just as a seismograph needs certain relatively immovable components in order to detect terrestrial shudders, a human being needs a more or less unvarying solidity of perception if he is to keep a healthy, properly amused sense of life's sometimes curious ways. In the beginning at least, I did not find it difficult to keep my perceptions from fluttering unsteadily in the winds that alternately buffeted and caressed me. (Whether they remained steady indefinitely, the reader will perhaps wish to judge for himself. Once celebrity seizes its quarry, the pressures toward change, no matter how strongly they may be resisted, are formidably seductive.)

Nor did I forget that much of my good fortune was a matter of nothing more clever on my part than luck. If, in any event, I had noticeably lost my sense of direction, someone or other would no doubt have obligingly cracked me on the knuckles and reminded me who I was and where I had come from. Any number of people, after all, including many I did not know, were as aware as I was of the role happenstance had played in guiding me to write my book at exactly the right moment. As Harvey Myman, a reviewer for a California newspaper, wrote, "It just so happens that the fates were exceedingly kind and saw fit to propel a moderately successful magazine editor and author into a superstar." Or as Larry Batson, a columnist for the *Minneapolis Tribune,* put it, "Fixx . . . is in something like the delightful predicament, described by Charles Lamb, of doing good by stealth and being discovered by accident. Fixx wrote a book on running simply because he loves it. It turned out that tens of thousands of people were waiting for just such a book."

The results of this happy surprise were more than

I or anyone else anticipated. *The Complete Book of Running* outsold almost every book then available, including every work of nonfiction my publisher had handled since he started business back in 1927. I was interviewed on talk shows in all the major cities in the United States, as well as in England, Australia and New Zealand. Reporters and photographers from newspapers and magazines visited my house. *People* magazine chose me, along with Meat Loaf, Jimmy Carter and such luminaries as Brooke Shields and Miss Piggy, as one of 1978's most intriguing people. In the course of all this I encountered, and occasionally became friends with, some of the most extraordinary (and in some cases unlikely) men and women the American way of life has managed to produce.

The prices of being well known, and not just the rewards, are necessarily part of this account. When one's life becomes markedly different from the lives of one's neighbors, a new field of force is created and the iron filings rearrange themselves to the far reaches of that field. No matter how much one may struggle against change, relationships alter. New friends (or are they?) appear. Old ones, for reasons that may not always be entirely clear, drift away. Even within one's closest family, affections shift.

Such changes are part of the oddness of celebrity, particularly when it arrives without warning. In the beginning, being well known is wonderful fun. Doors previously closed are suddenly and spectacularly open. Invitations arrive, astonishing the recipient with opportunity, flattery and largesse. A trip to Paris on the Concorde? A cruise on the *QE2*? Name it; it's yours. On streets and at airports, heads turn and autographs are solicited.

It is, however, impossible to be unaware that celebrity, no matter how diluted, shimmers with ambiguities and incongruities. I could hardly fail to notice, for example, that after the appearance of *The Complete Book of Running* my writing was more sought after than previously, even though it was unlikely that it had improved significantly over what I had been routinely turning out for the previous two decades. Similarly, my opinions on subjects ranging from sports to the future of the Western world were now prized, or at least inquired into. One interviewer startled me by asking, "Will civilization as we know it survive the century?" ("No," I told him and watched as, without comment, he soberly wrote down my reply.)

No matter how well known you are, however, you can never be certain at any given moment just what price your fame will fetch. Like the franc, fame floats, fluctuating in value not just from day to day but from moment to moment. One day I stood in line at a ticket counter in Washington's National Airport. Ahead of me, arranging for a flight, was a woman whose name and face are familiar to anyone who has ever watched a television talk show. Having handed the agent a check, she was routinely asked for some means of identification. With a condescending smile she loftily pointed to her name. The agent replied politely, "I'm sorry. It's airline policy to require identification for all checks." She finally capitulated and provided what he asked. She had overestimated, at least in National Airport, the magnitude and leverage of her renown. After my book had been at the top of the chief bestseller lists for several weeks, an acquaintance with a weakness for vivid phrases told me, "You're hot as a firecracker." He was, of course, wrong. When a firecracker is hot, it's hot all over. Human incandescence is rarely that uniform.

Soon after *The Complete Book of Running* appeared, for example, the Quaker Oats Company asked me if I would be willing to make some television commercials for one of its breakfast cereals. A one-year contract was drawn up, signed and subsequently renewed for two twelve-month periods. When it was finally about to expire, a representative of Quaker's advertising agency, Michael Gallant, telephoned me to request an additional six-month extension. To my surprise, however, he offered considerably less than my previous fee. I asked why my stipend had been so sharply reduced. "You're not as popular as you once were," he explained.

Such tantalizing ambiguities reached their clearest expression one January afternoon as I lay, unshaven and wearing a pair of faded blue jeans, watching the Pittsburgh Steelers and the Dallas Cowboys in the Super Bowl game. A whistle blew and a quarter ended. Suddenly there I was on the television screen, jogging past the Eiffel Tower and the Seine in an American Express commercial I had made several months earlier. Who was I? Was I the sleepy, unkempt man lying there on the couch, or the public person whose commercial had just been witnessed by a hundred million viewers? That afternoon I was out of focus even to myself.

Such puzzlements suggest why fame deserves a more rigorous and searching sociology than it has thus far enjoyed. If for no other reason than its rarity, there is much about renown that remains unfathomed and that thus provides abundant scope for investigation. What I have done in these pages, therefore, I have done at least partly in a spirit of bemused inquiry. I have tried to specify, as truthfully as I could, exactly what the voyage was like for one explorer, and what, rightly or wrongly, he was able to conclude about its meanings not just for celebrities but for all of us. For celebrity, by its nature, is never a solitary phenomenon. It is a contractual relationship, one that requires not just an actor but a willing audience as well.

Had someone else been the protagonist of this adventure, the plot would no doubt have taken a different turn. For one thing, given its authorship, my book's success was, as I have suggested, a considerable surprise. If a gambler had wanted to bet on a winning horse, I would hardly have been the horse to bet on. I am characteristically indolent, unambitious, disdainful of money and success, and, despite long immersion in a society that prizes competitiveness and what in the more bellicose circles of business is called aggressiveness, perversely noncompetitive and unaggressive. Some years ago, when I was a junior staff member at *Saturday Review,* a colleague predicted that I would never go far on the magazine because in the eyes of its restlessly energetic editor, Norman Cousins, I badly lacked "zoom." Though partly a jest, the comment was mostly true. I *did* lack zoom, among other qualities.

I also lacked, in important particulars, the kind of pedigree usually found in winners. My paternal grandfather, Henry Fix (my father added the second *x,* on grounds that a person's name ought to be a proper noun, not a verb), was a logger. I met him just once, when I was four years old, and have only one photograph of him. A lanky man with dour eyes, he is belted near the tip of a fir tree in western Washington. Leaning precariously backward, his boot cleats anchored in bark, he saws patiently at the topmost wisp of trunk. His wife, my grandmother, worked as a telephone operator in Elma, a town in the countryside west of Olympia that to this day has a population of fewer than two thousand souls.

My maternal grandfather, who was raised in Colorado, was a lawyer and businessman who prac-

ticed law for only two unspectacular years and at
business did poorly, or at best spottily. When World
War II ended he involved himself with a company that
planned to turn military surplus to civilian uses. He
once showed me a toy truck the firm had managed to
fashion out of a metal gas mask cannister. It wasn't
much of a truck, or for that matter much of a toy. My
grandfather, whom I called Pop-pop, was a constant
and beloved part of my young life; I held him in awed
reverence. He built a country house where I spent my
first thirteen or fourteen summers, and where I
learned to fish for bass, shoot a rifle and climb back
onto a horse after it had thrown me with bone-jarring
force against a stone wall. He could bake cherry and
blueberry cobbler and was able to distinguish good
from bad watermelons by rapping them with his
knuckles and appraising the reverberations of the
rinds. He had many excellent qualities, including tenacious industry, but worldly success was nowhere
among them.

When I was three or four years old my family lived
in a walk-up apartment in Long Island City, across the
East River from midtown Manhattan. Then, as now,
Long Island City was mostly factories, railroad yards,
piers, noise and soot. To anyone familiar with it in
those days, calling any part of it run-down would be
an egregious redundancy. At night, even through
drawn shades, the walls of my bedroom vibrated with
orange flickers from a neon SUNSHINE sign that deco-
rated the whitewashed flank of an adjacent commercial bakery. Later we moved to Corona, a few subway
stops farther out on Long Island. Several blocks away,
on the waterfront, was a garbage dump of many acres
that was a fine place for a child to hunt for treasure.
In time, however, progress came even to the dump.
The runways for LaGuardia Airport's inconceivably

immense DC-3's were poured there and another place of childhood enchantment was gone.

Our landlord in Corona, Mr. Mazzeo, had a basement roomful of wine and sausage, all homemade and all of wondrously unforgettable pungency. We lived in his building during the Great Depression. My father did typing, researching and odd jobs for a writer and anthologist named Alfred Kreymborg. Once, at another writer's apartment, he met William Faulkner. Of the meeting he wrote to a friend: "I am reading the manuscript of a novel by Bill Faulkner.* He is from the South and is up here about something connected with a couple of books Harcourt Brace are publishing of his. This is one of them. He seems a very decent fellow. He writes something like Hemingway (his descriptions) and Joyce (the flow of thought and introspective business). Anyway, his stuff sounds damn good. I was astonished the other day when he said he had only been writing since 1924. He is about thirty-two years old. He says he's tried a few short stories but they're too long; there's something wrong with them."

In 1936 our fortunes began to improve. In that year my father found a job at *Time* and, with it, a modest prosperity that enabled us to move away from Corona. At *Time* he met and became friends with such journalists as James Agee, Whittaker Chambers, T. S. Matthews and Eric Hodgins. It was Hodgins, the author of *Mr. Blandings Builds His Dream House,* who, when my father had a heart attack and was advised to recuperate in a warm climate, suggested that he spend the winter in Sarasota, Florida, a suggestion that was to influence my own life more than I suspected. For it was there, working during summer vacations in the greasy clutter at Austin's Texaco Service on the South Tami-

*Probably *Sartoris* or *The Sound and the Fury.*

ami Trail, that I first enjoyed what was to be a long and amiable relationship with such earthy practicalities as brake drums, wrenches and fingernails that will not come clean no matter how diligently they are scrubbed.

Though uncomfortably cognizant, in *Time*'s humming hive of Ivy League men, of his lack of a college education, my father created a place for himself, and his name is mentioned in several books about the period. In his autobiographical *Name and Address,* T. S. Matthews, who was for several years managing editor of *Time,* describes my father's arrival at the book review department. "It was [Robert] Cantwell who got us an assistant, a slightly older friend of his named Calvin Fixx, who came from the Northwest, and who had introduced him to the writing of Henry James. He was a clear-sighted man, wise beyond his years, and a good friend. When he died I missed him sadly, and *Time* was a poorer place." In an essay on James Agee, Robert Fitzgerald referred to my father during this period as "a Mormon [he was not, nor had he ever been], a decent, luminously inarticulate man." Finally, in *Witness,* Whittaker Chambers remembered him as "one of the wisest, gentlest and mellowest souls I will ever know." Chambers continues, "Often we ended our week at four o'clock in the morning after having worked for thirty-six hours, almost without stopping and wholly without sleep. We kept up the pace by smoking five or six packs of cigarettes and drinking thirteen or fourteen cups of coffee a day."

When he was forty-three years old my father died of a heart attack; it was exactly seven years after his first attack. I was seventeen and in my senior year of high school, the most unsettled and self-centered phase of an adolescence that still makes me wince in embarrassment when I think of much of it. Partly because of my singleminded preoccupation with my own confusions, I never knew my father as well as I wish I had. He was not just a wise man but a good one, and I learned more from him than he knew. One thing I did not learn from him, however, and could not because it was, I believe, nowhere in him, was an instinct for going for life's jugular, for craving something badly enough to raise hell in order to get it. When spectacular good fortune did eventually arrive, therefore, it did so almost entirely in spite of my ambitions and inclinations.

If there was a parental influence prodding me toward achievement, or at least making achievement seem more plausible than not, it was, I think, my mother's. She simply did not—and to this day does not—acknowledge limits, conventions or categories for herself or for anyone else; she has an eye for possibilities rather than impediments. In fact, as I write these words she is enrolled, a student of seventy-three, in a university course on British writing, amused but nonplussed at being a full half-century older than any other student in the class. Freud remarks, "A man who has been the indisputable favorite of his mother keeps for life the feeling of a conqueror, that confidence of success which frequently induces real success." My mother always seemed evenhanded in her attentions to my sister and me. Nonetheless, while I was growing up I felt, much of the time anyhow, as if my mother showed me noticeably more attention and, equally important, more respect than was common among the mothers of my contemporaries.

When, therefore, success of a sort finally came, it seemed neither so surprising nor so awesome as it otherwise might have. Although I was unprepared for many of its manifestations, I felt merely surprised rather than overwhelmed. Once, in Los Angeles, I found myself signing autographs for two full hours.

Giving and receiving autographs is a curious transaction, a symbolic ceding of some value in oneself, and I have never found myself in that relationship without wondering what prize the recipients suppose themselves to be acquiring. Yet, puzzled as I was that finger-numbing afternoon, it did not once occur to me to declare my fraudulence and call it a day. I figured I probably wasn't much more fraudulent than anyone else would have been under the same circumstances.

There were other ways in which an observer might have judged me unlikely to slip easily into success. I was, and still am, conspicuously stubborn. The surest way to persuade me to do exactly what you want me to do is to urge me to do something else. At Trinity School in the late 1940s, students were indoctrinated in the virtues of energetic participation in the various after-class programs; those of us who left the building at the two-thirty bell instead of lingering for sports, glee club rehearsals or general ingratiation with the faculty were stigmatized as "two-thirty strollers." Except during the tennis season, when I dutifully remained for practice, I was the most incorrigible of such miscreants. "Fixx," the headmaster once told me, "you have an unfortunate tendency to be an individual."

His assessment was nowhere more convincingly corroborated than in my willful recalcitrance toward that most central of all Trinity School activities: athletics. Although I played baseball and football when I couldn't avoid it, I had almost no interest in such sports. Tennis was the game I enjoyed most, particularly when it was singles and most especially when I was behind and could relish the solitary challenge of figuring out, in consultation with only my own wits and wiles, how to improve a losing game. Had a tennis genie, emerging in an obliging puff of smoke from a can of Spaldings, offered to reveal to me the secrets of winning, I would have declined his counsel. For better or worse I liked, and still like, being on my own. So far as I know, no one, in sport or anywhere else, has ever mistaken me for a team player.

Nor did my attitudes toward money do anything to stimulate my ambitions. When I was a child, money was seldom mentioned, either by my family or my friends, and it thus never occupied much of a place in my mind. Growing up amid the ever-present commercial bustle of New York City, I could scarcely fail to be aware that many people gave money considerably more attention than we did, but such comparative anthropology did little to influence my view about what constituted a proper attitude toward it. Quite clearly, the right attitude was one of amused disdain. Nice people simply didn't talk, or even think, about money.

I had at least one other limitation, and this one was psychological. Moreover, even though I understood it quite clearly, there was for a long time little I could do about it, or wanted to. After my father's death it seemed a disloyalty to seek to surpass his accomplishments, and anyway there was no need to; he had, after all, done well enough. In my work, therefore, I customarily affected a bemused insouciance. Only once, so far as I know, did anyone penetrate the pose. A dozen years ago I coolly quit a well-paying magazine job. Because the company I worked for, the McCall Corporation, was in a period of turmoil, my boss's boss, the industrialist David Mahoney, visited my office and urged me to stay on rather than further roil turbulent waters. "If you leave," he told me ominously, "you'll be ruining your entire career. I guarantee it." I left just the same. Soon afterward a friend, shaking his head, commented, "You're some blithe spirit, Fixx. I just hope those easygoing ways of yours don't get you into trouble one of these days."

My easygoing ways disappeared, quite suddenly, in 1975. During that year, on Shakespeare's birthday, I became forty-three years old, the age my father had been when he died. Thereafter it no longer struck me as unseemly or disrespectful to try to do more than he had done. Soon, after all, I would be older than he was —older than my own father! I felt a new freedom to work more purposefully than I previously had. It didn't bother me any more if people noticed that I was unabashedly trying to hit home runs. It was during this year that I started writing *The Complete Book of Running.*

Reading over what I have set down so far, I see that I may have given the impression that I was so way- ward, so psychologically handicapped and so gener- ally ineffectual that only charity or a miracle could ever have brought me a day's pay. Of course, this was not quite the case. Several aspects of background and temperament, in fact, offered me considerable suste- nance when I finally decided to quit fooling around and get down to work.

Even as a child, for one thing, I had friends with striking, and in some cases strikingly well developed, literary interests. In the public grammar school I at- tended, a fellow sixth-grader wrote a good-sized ad- venture novel. Although I no longer remember details of its plot, I was greatly impressed by the inch-thick pile of manuscript he accumulated. At the age of twelve or thirteen a friend, who later was to write for *Time* and then for *Newsweek,* introduced me to the works of H. L. Mencken. Finally, a close companion during practically all my high school years, an in- candescently puckish green-eyed neighbor named Peggy, wrote poetry that many adult poets might have envied. It was not at all a bad atmosphere for a writer to grow up in.

I started writing for my own amusement long before I was out of grammar school. The first essay I can remember, a fanciful speculation on how racial characteristics influence musical composition, contained the words "emotional outlet." I showed it to my father and asked if he didn't think the phrase too glib. No, he said, it seemed fine to him. I knew he was taking it easy on me.

It was not, however, until I entered Oberlin College and, to help meet expenses, took a $25-a-week job as a part-time reporter at the town weekly, the *Oberlin News-Tribune,* that I began to acquire a sense of what it means to be professional in one's writing. One morning, following a late party the night before, a hangover of unrelenting malevolence molested my skull as I sat at my noisy old Underwood. It was a Wednesday, and the *News-Tribune,* like most country weeklies, went to press that night, so the story I was writing could not be postponed. Next day, recovered, I read it in print. To my surprise it secmed about the same as what I customarily wrote when I felt fine. I had discovered that in order to write decently I didn't have to wait for the muses.

However, none of this seemed to me or to anyone else like the sort of thing best sellers are made of. Nor did much that happened to me during the next decade and a half. At the age of twenty-six, having worked briefly for a Florida daily and then a Manhattan publishing house, I was hired as articles editor of *Saturday Review.* Norman Cousins, the magazine's editor, had as quick and agile a mind as I had ever encountered, and he did not waste time if he could help it. To this day I can quote my pre-employment interview verbatim:

COUSINS: Can you write?
FIXX: Yes.
COUSINS: Can you edit?
FIXX: Yes.
COUSINS: Can you write headlines?
FIXX: Yes.
COUSINS: Do you want to work for *Saturday Review*?
FIXX: I certainly do.
COUSINS: When can you start?

It turned out that I was good with a pencil and had a knack for making flabby prose publishable. The strongest ideas for articles, however, typically came from other members of the staff, most often Cousins himself, and because of my inadequacies in that respect my reign as a boy wonder was brief.

Furthermore, I not infrequently found myself puzzled by Cousins's genius. Once he asked me to read the manuscript of an editorial he had written. It was a proposal for the founding of an organization to be called the Society for Individual Responsibility, and Cousins had titled the editorial simply "S.I.R." Having read it, I offered two observations. First, I told him, the acronym was misleading; S.I.R. sounded like a men's club. Second, I pointed out, the idea itself contained an inherent contradiction. It is not, after all, exactly individual responsibility if you need to join a society to exercise it.

Cousins, smiling knowingly, went ahead and published the editorial, title and all, just about as he had written it. It appealed to our readers so strongly that we had to hire several temporary assistants to answer the mail from applicants clamoring to exercise their individual responsibility by signing up as S.I.R. members.

It was something of a surprise, therefore, when, in 1967, Cousins offered me a promotion: the editorship of *McCall's,* of which he was a director. Of course I was pleased. *McCall's* had the third largest circulation among American magazines (only *Reader's Digest* and *TV Guide* were more widely read), and at first I found the job fascinating. But I soon discovered that running the magazine was in many respects not journalism at all. It consisted of interminable meetings, adjudications and delvings into circulation figures, budgets and such recurrent chores as deciding how much each writer and editor ought to be paid. Late one afternoon, as I was putting on my coat to leave for the day, a young staff member appeared in my office. She was sobbing, having just learned that she would not after all receive a raise she had been counting on. She explained that she and her husband, a graduate student, had recently picked out some new furniture at Bloomingdale's and now, unable to pay for it, would have to cancel their order. We talked. She cried and pleaded. Outside, it was getting dark. The lights along Park Avenue came on. By the time I was finally able to go, it was late and I was hungry. I wondered what kind of work this was for a journalist. I knew of no remedy, however. At *Life,* whose staff I later joined, I tried to leaven my executive responsibilities with occasional writing, but this proved a self-defeating solution; it only meant that I was neglecting the work the magazine had hired me to do.

For nearly ten years, therefore, I was bored and restless. The work I was doing wasn't what I wanted to do, and I therefore did not do it very well. It was during this period that I came across a magazine article about "flame-out," the phenomenon that occurs when a career loses forward thrust, like a jet aircraft with engine failure. I was startled. The article seemed to describe me exactly. I had no idea, furthermore, whether I would discover a way to restart my engine. After

McCall's and *Life* I found inconsequential freelance assignments at the *New York Times* and *Reader's Digest* and, later, editorial posts at *Audience,* a meticulously edited magazine that failed after thirteen issues, and at *Horizon.* In early 1975, after I had puzzled for months over what unfathomable laws, natural or unnatural, lay behind the workings of *Horizon,* my boss, Shirley Tomkievicz, took me to lunch one day and told me she thought I ought to consider leaving.

Although by this time I had little interest in looking for another magazine job, I knew of no other way to earn a living—at least not the sort of living I needed. I had a mortgaged house, four children and a wife, not to mention a former wife, for whom I was required to provided some $12,000 a year.

At about this time a call from Pyke Johnson, my editor at Doubleday, helped me move in a direction I could not otherwise have taken. Three years earlier I had published a collection of puzzles called *Games for the Superintelligent.* A sequel, *More Games for the Superintelligent,* was now ready for the press. Having been offered the second book as a potential selection, the Book-of-the-Month Club had unexpectedly taken its predecessor as well and had paid a $10,000 advance. It occurred to me, therefore, that if I could interest Doubleday in publishing a third book of mine, and could persuade the firm to pay me an advance of perhaps $10,000 against whatever royalties the sales would ultimately bring, I might in that way assemble enough money to keep me going for a while. Ultimately, I knew, it would probably be necessary to return to magazine work, but in the meantime I would have had an agreeable respite.

The chief problem was what sort of idea to offer Doubleday. My first two books, which I had written in odd hours while working at full-time jobs, had brought advances of $4,000 and $6,000. Since, however, I now had no other income, I needed a larger advance than these. Therefore I saw that I had to come up with an idea that would be likely to sell fairly well.

It was at this point that the notion of writing a book about running occurred to me. It was evident that interest in the sport was growing. I myself had started running seven or eight years earlier in order to repair a calf muscle pulled while changing direction too abruptly on a tennis court. In the beginning, this was my only goal, and I ran only occasionally in its pursuit —a mile or two whenever it occurred to me. Nonetheless, before I had been at it for many weeks I observed several unexpected side effects. Without trying, I lost weight. I felt more energetic. For some reason I drank less. When I visited my doctor, he told me, in a puzzled tone, that I seemed healthier than I had in years.

I noticed some surprising psychological benefits as well. I was calmer, less readily distressed by crisis and pressure. (Researchers have since demonstrated that running's calming effects are not unlike those of tranquilizers, except that there are no undesirable side effects.) I felt cheerful, buoyant and optimistic. Work seemed easier and play more fun.

In short, I suspected that there was more to running than most people, even most experts, knew. I therefore began drafting an outline under the working title *The Lazy Athlete's Look Younger Be Thinner Feel Better & Live Longer Running Book.* As I envisioned it, the book would be breezy, superficial and easy to write. Since publishers' advances are customarily paid in two installments—half when a contract is signed, the rest when the manuscript is accepted—a quickly written book would bring the money in that much more promptly.

At about this time I had a conversation that turned a modest and easily manageable plan into a two-year obsession. At *Horizon* one of my final duties was to ask the novelist Jerzy Kosinski to write an essay for the magazine. One afternoon, as Kosinski and I sat talking in his studio in midtown Manhattan, the conversation turned to my book.

"You have a big job ahead of you," Kosinski said. "To write a book like that, you have to read everything that's been written on the subject."

Until then I hadn't thought of doing anything of the sort. All I wanted to do was get the book written quickly and collect my check from Doubleday. Gradually I realized that Kosinski was right. Exhaustive research would not only give my book a greater specific gravity than is common in sports books but would make it more interesting to write. I therefore abandoned the first outline and wrote a new one. In it I said:

> Although many people are unaware of it, the jogging fad of five or six years ago has finally blossomed into a major boom. . . . Nonetheless, there is thus far no general book on the subject—no book that tells you everything you need to know to get started, become fit, stay that way, and deal with the problems and pleasures you encounter. There are, of course, books that take up limited aspects of running, but there is nothing that gathers it all—both the practice of running and its spirit—together in one place. . . .

It was at this point that my adventures began. The following pages, closely based on my daily journals as well as on letters, clippings and other documents, consist of some of the more telling anecdotes and incidents that comprised those adventures. Except for an occasional name that has been charitably disguised and several minor adjustments in chronology, they are, no matter how improbable they seem, faithful to what actually happened.

When I started keeping my journals several years ago, I had no thought of ever using them as the basis for a book; they were too private for that, and too unguarded. Reflection has persuaded me, however, that my experience has been so tantalizingly unusual that a value is likely to be served by relating it—the good, the bad, the regrettable and the just plain silly —pretty much as it happened. I am aware, of course, that in pursuit of this purpose I have in more than one instance done violence to the customary rules of propriety. I have been indecently specific about money earned, triumphs enjoyed and anxieties endured, and in a few passages, when it seemed germane, I have with willful impoliteness told tales out of school.

For none of these transgressions do I feel inclined to make apology. There is, after all, a value inherent in relating the truth—any truth—about human experience. This seems to me particularly so when the experience is one not all of us are able to enjoy at first hand, and more especially when it suggests that money and renown, which are so singlemindedly and energetically sought after by so many of us, are really not anything like what they are commonly imagined to be.

II

"Who in the World Will Want to Read a Book About Running?"

April 19, 1976

Last week I mailed the outline to Pyke Johnson at
Doubleday, along with a letter politely asking for
$10,000. Everyone says that's not much of an advance
in these inflationary times—the really big writers routinely get six figures. Still, it sounds like plenty to me.

A letter arrives from Johnson today. He says he's
interested. He invites me to come to the Doubleday
offices next week to discuss my idea with Sandy Richardson, Doubleday's editor-in-chief.

An enclosure that comes with Johnson's letter confuses me, however. It is an advertisement, clipped
from a magazine, for a collection of essays and articles

about running that another publisher brought out some time ago. The advertisement reports that 25,000 copies are in print. Johnson's implication in sending it to me, I conclude, is that with so many copies of such a book already in existence, the market may be saturated. It is not an encouraging sign.

April 26

We meet in Richardson's office on Park Avenue. The room is piled high with newly published Doubleday books.

"We're enthusiastic about your book," Richardson begins. "If we give it a catchy title, such as *The Joy of Running,* it could do quite well." He is amiable and expansive. I tell him I am pleased.

"There are some problems, however," he continues. Thereupon he spends several minutes describing the difficulties my idea presents for Doubleday. "To be perfectly candid," he says, "we don't feel that a book on a sport like running has much sales potential. Furthermore, your name isn't widely known. If, say, you were Frank Shorter, we would be assured of a market. As it is, a book by you will require a large promotional budget in order to let readers know who you are."

What these difficulties add up to, Richardson explains, is that while Doubleday is willing to advance me the $10,000, it cannot, unfortunately, offer me nearly as high a royalty rate as I enjoyed for *Games for the Superintelligent* and *More Games for the Superintelligent.*

I am not just discouraged by the meeting but puzzled too. It seems odd that, having written two books for Doubleday that sold well, I should now in effect find myself demoted. If I can avoid it, I don't want to leave the firm for another publisher. On the other hand, Doubleday's offer could conceivably mean a lot less money than I would earn under a better contract with another house.

It is clear that I need advice.

April 27

I telephone Julian Bach, a New York literary agent whose clients include a number of best-selling authors, among them Theodore H. White, Nathan Pritikin and Robert Elegant. Over the years, as a magazine editor, I have had occasion to publish articles by several of Bach's clients and have been impressed by his honesty and intelligence. He invites me to drop by his office day after tomorrow.

April 29

The Bach agency occupies a handful of cheerfully cluttered second-floor rooms in the Scribners Building on Fifth Avenue at Forty-eighth Street.* A pleasant, urbane man who once worked as an editor at *Life,* Bach directs me to an antique settee. I have to move several boxed manuscripts aside in order to find a place to sit.

I hand him a memorandum outlining Doubleday's proposal. He reads it and, shaking his head, says, "It's not very good, is it?" If I don't want to accept the Doubleday offer, he suggests, I have several choices: I can try, on my own, to get Doubleday to improve the offer; I can have him or some other agent negotiate with Doubleday on my behalf; or, finally, I can see whether another publisher might be willing to offer a better contract.

Having no confidence in my ability to conduct negotiations with a publisher, I tell Bach I will be

*It has since moved to a new office building on Third Avenue, a few blocks to the east.

grateful if he will see what he can persuade Doubleday to do.

May 3

Bach telephones. The news, he tells me, is discouraging. Doubleday is willing to make only insignificant concessions. I therefore ask him reluctantly to see what interest, if any, other publishers may have.

May 11

Bach calls again. An editor at Random House, Joe Fox, has made an offer. The advance, because I felt I needed no more to live on, is the same as that offered by Doubleday—$10,000—but the royalty rate is considerably higher. If the book were to sell 30,000 copies, a decent but by no means spectacular performance, I calculate that I would earn $10,625 more under the Random House contract than under Doubleday's.

I tell Bach I think I had better sign with Random House.

He says he agrees; a contract will now be drawn up.

May 22

Alice and I attend a party in Manhattan. A woman I know, the wife of a magazine writer, asks what I am doing these days.

"I've just started work on a book," I reply.

"How nice," she says brightly. "On what subject?" I tell her.

"*Running?*" she exclaims pityingly. "Who in the world will want to read a book about running?"

June 2

A friend who works in publishing tells me he has just heard that an athletic San Diego psychiatrist, Thaddeus Kostrubala, will soon come out with a book called *The Joy of Running*. There goes my title. Although I am aware, having written a great many headlines for magazine articles, that for any piece of writing there is almost no limit to the potentially usable titles, the news is upsetting just the same. Like Johnson and Richardson, both Fox and I thought *The Joy of Running* was exactly right for my book.

I telephone Fox and tell him the bad news. He suggests *The Complete Book of Running* instead.

I ask him, "What do you think of *Come Run with Me?*"

"It's a perfectly terrible title," he says.

I'm smart enough to know when to surrender. I tell him *The Complete Book of Running* sounds fine.*

June 3–July 30

With Jerzy Kosinski's advice in mind I start reading everything I can find on running, including some of the planet's most impenetrable scientific prose. (Doctors, for some reason, are either very good writers—Lewis Thomas, Michael Crichton, Somerset Maugham—or else they are dreadful.) I conduct interviews in California, Indiana, Boston and New Jersey. I tape conversations, make notes. My files, arranged in folders labeled with working titles of the twenty-four chapters I plan to write, soon fill half a dozen cardboard grocery cartons.

My sister, Kitty, comes down from Boston one day for a visit. Seeing the chaos of books, documents and tape cassettes in my study, she suggests that I need a filing cabinet—either that or a broom. I know she is

*Several months later, at a medical conference, I finally meet Kostrubala and tease him about having stolen my title. He tells me he would just as soon I had used *The Joy of Running*; he never much liked it, with its archly playful echo of *The Joy of Sex*. An editor, he says, dreamed it up over a martini lunch one day, mostly in jest, and it simply stuck.

right, but I am too busy to clean up. The book has turned into a tyranny. In a letter to a friend I apologize for having become such a recluse:

> The book is so much on my mind that it crowds all else out and will, I fear, for a while. You see, my plan is simply to make it so complete that no one will have any reason to do anything like it for a long, long time. That's why I go to such pains to get absolutely everything into it, no matter how much effort it takes. I could write a perfectly good book right now if I would let myself do it, but I need to be much better stocked with information (and with thoughts) before I try. I haven't written a word yet.

I encounter a problem. I had told Fox that one chapter in the book would be a report on what happens when a mediocre, middle-of-the-pack athlete—specifically, me—runs side by side with a champion. I therefore write to Frank Shorter, an Olympic gold medalist in 1972 and silver medalist in 1976, asking if I might come out to his home in Boulder, Colorado, and spend some time with him. I receive no answer.

I write a second time. Again Shorter does not reply.

I send another letter. Still nothing.

Reporting my failure to Fox, I say, "I guess I'll just have to skip that chapter."

"I think that would be a mistake," he says. "It will make a strong part of the book. How about getting Bill Rodgers?"

I telephone Rodgers, who at the time has won only one major race, the 1975 Boston Marathon.

"Sure, come on up whenever you want to," he says.

August 5

Rodgers and his wife, Ellen, live in a small rented apartment on the top floor of a frame house in Melrose, Massachusetts, a suburb just north of Boston.

They own a rusting Volkswagen, and their bathtub shower, where I clean up after Rodgers and I have run nine miles together, consists of cracked rubber tubing guyed with wrapping twine. The Rodgerses, who are schoolteachers, are hospitable, serving warm chocolate chip cookies and ginger ale during our interview. It is a pleasant afternoon, and in *The Complete Book of Running* it will form the basis for a chapter.*

August 16–September 7

I have started writing. I am describing the effect of exercise on the heart. The words I am writing seem to me to contain an inherent, even though largely invisible, falsity. It is that I have never seen a human heart.

I ask two friends who are doctors if they know where I can find a heart. The only ones they are aware of, they tell me, are in use and are thus not readily accessible for inspection.

One day I fly to Muncie, Indiana, to interview David Costill, a physiology researcher, and a colleague, Bud Getchell. I mention to Getchell my misgivings about describing the function of something I have not seen.

Getchell smiles. "Follow me," he says.

He takes me into a room containing a clutter of scientific apparatus. Standing against a wall is an old refrigerator. He opens it and removes a jar. In it, preserved in a fluid that smells unpleasant, is a man's heart. It has yellowed and looks flabby and rancid. While its owner was alive one of the heart's openings

---

*The encounter, it turns out, is luckier than I realized at the time, for soon afterward Rodgers, blossoming, begins to win almost every race he enters. Meanwhile, plagued by injury, Shorter never again runs as well as he had. After the book is published a friend asks me, "How did you happen to be smart enough to base that chapter on Rodgers instead of Shorter? At the time I thought you were crazy." I just smile and look wise.

was fitted with a thimble-sized mechanical device made of white plastic and bright wire. Someone had stitched it to the heart with a geometric tracery of threads. It is an artificial valve.

Getchell invites me to touch the heart. Timidly, I poke at it with a forefinger. It yields, as veal Parmesan might.

From now on I expect to write about hearts with an easier conscience.

Working on the book brings another difficulty. It is that in describing my own running experiences I know I need to be wary of sounding excessively satisfied with what I have done: lost sixty pounds, run ten miles a day for a decade, competed in twenty marathons (including Boston several times), and so forth. Five years ago, having run in my first major marathon, I wrote a magazine article on the experience. On that occasion I was so busy trying to conceal my pride behind a toe-scuffing diffidence (entirely feigned) that the piece seemed to me noticeably uneven despite a good deal of fiddling with its tone. In *The Complete Book of Running*, therefore, I decide simply to let myself go and act as delighted with my participation in the sport as I really am, in the hope that readers, sensing that my enthusiasm is honest, will forgive its unrestrained exuberance.*

For as many years as I can remember, I have spent most of my working time with other people. Now,

---

*It will perhaps already have occurred to the reader that the present book is subject to a similar difficulty. On the one hand, since its author's experiences have conformed so closely to at least one version of the American dream, he is pleased to have had them. On the other, he is apprehensively aware that he had better not seem *too* pleased—or at least too *obviously* pleased.

except when I am interviewing authorities like David Costill and Bud Getchell, I work alone.

I do my writing in an upstairs room that is scarcely bigger than a packing crate and, in winter, not much warmer. The desk I use, black steel with a surface of imitation-walnut Formica, is no larger than a welcome mat, and was once the domain of the Puerto Rican mail clerk, Eddie, at *Audience* magazine. People who visit my study and see Eddie's diminutive desk invariably remark on how spartan my working quarters are. Nonetheless, I like it here. I have a shelf stocked with reference books. I also have three typewriters, an electric pencil sharpener, and an FM radio to listen to when I am feeling self-indulgent—everything, in short, that the well-equipped anchorite could possibly need.

Knowing I have not always worked in such a solitary manner, friends occasionally ask me if I have trouble summoning the necessary self-discipline to keep at it. I tell them that I do not. It is the truth. Remembering the trials of working at *McCall's, Life* and *Horizon* would in itself be enough to keep me content here in my monk's cell. In addition, however, I find, somewhat to my surprise, that I very much like the rhythm of a day spent alone.

Alice, who runs her own public relations company in Manhattan, leaves after breakfast. Thereupon such children as may at the time be on vacation from school depart—Paul to install Dictograph burglar alarms in local offices and homes, John to work as a busboy (and eventually, having been promoted, a waiter) at Manero's Steak House, Stephen to his post at the Riverside Texaco station. (Some families—the Rockefellers, the Lodges, the Roosevelts—devote themselves, generation after generation, to public service; we Fixxes seem to give perpetual allegiance to Texaco.) The rest of the day now lies before me, uninterrupted except for phone calls, the mail's arrival at noon, a late-afternoon run, and the intermittent visits of the local Electrolux representative, a gentleman whose ungrudging acceptance of rebuff is an example of forbearance deserving of emulation by us all.

For three or four hours I write, doing first drafts in longhand; the purr of No. 2 graphite on notebook paper gives the words an aural lushness, a sensual second dimension, that my Smith-Corona does not. At noon I stop for lunch and read the mail. Afterward I go back upstairs or, in good weather, into the backyard to work at a bench under the tall blue spruce that grows there. It is a peaceful and pleasant way to spend a day.

Perhaps the chief drawback is that some of the neighbors, seeing me around when other men are at their jobs, assume I am at home because I am unable to find work. A year or two ago a man who lives nearby lost his job. Fearful that his ten-year-old daughter, to whom he is prodigiously devoted, might suffer anxieties, he continued to leave his house each morning at the customary hour, boarded a commuter train for Manhattan, and simply walked around, killing the day, until it was time to come home for supper. Out of work for a year, he adhered to this routine, without a day's deviation, during the entire period.

Evidently some people think that I, too, am out of work. A compassionate, churchgoing woman who lives down the street has taken to reading the want ads in the local daily, the *Greenwich Time*, and passing promising leads along to me. One day she tells me that she understands real estate salespeople are greatly in demand. Not wanting to seem unappreciative of her generosity, I say that, like her, I am something of a student of the Connecticut economy and find its workings unfailingly interesting whenever I am able to take time from my writing to give it the attention it deserves.

She all but rolls her eyes in disbelief. It is as if I had told her that the FBI regularly broadcasts instructions to me through the fillings in my molars.

September 9

Joe Fox and I are talking. The book's scheduled publication date is still a year and a half away. In the parks and on the roads and trails where I run, I tell him, it is increasingly plain that the sport is no longer just a pastime but has become a movement. A year earlier, if I spent an hour running in Central Park, I might encounter a dozen fellow runners; now I routinely pass half a hundred.

Fox says, "I wish we had your book ready to publish right now."

He sees the concern on my face. It may be, I am thinking, that interest in running has already peaked or for that matter is even declining.

"Don't worry," Fox reassures me. "Your book will be just fine when we bring it out in early 1978."

I wonder. If running turns out to be only a fad, will it hold still long enough for us to get the book out before the enthusiasm withers away? Augmenting my anxieties is the fact that two other books on running, both by knowledgeable authorities, are scheduled to appear at about the same time as mine.*

By next year, running may not only be of little

*The books are George Sheehan's *Running and Being* and Bob Glover and Jack Shepherd's *The Runner's Handbook,* and both will be best sellers. In the early days of the running-book boom, there were readers aplenty. Today, of course, with several hundred books on the subject in print, the competition for attention is more vigorous and best sellers are accordingly rarer.

interest to anyone. It may also be overcrowded with a swarm of competing books.

I ask Fox how early he would need to have the manuscript in order to bring the book out in time for Christmas.

"We'd need it by February first," he replies. "But don't even try. There's no way you can make it."

He's probably right. Still, I decide to try anyway and see what happens. Accelerating my schedule, I begin working on the book twelve and sometimes fourteen hours a day.

January 31, 1977

Six months ahead of schedule, I turn the manuscript in to Fox, taking my sons John and Stephen along to underscore, if only for myself, the ceremonial significance of the occasion. I have, after all, done what Fox said could not be done: finished the book early enough to get it out before next Christmas.

Fox says he plans to read it right away. I am apprehensive. I have already discovered that he does not shrink from telling authors what he thinks. If he decides I have done poorly he will say so.

February 7–14

Fox telephones. Thank God, he likes what I have done. He tells me, however, that he has had his assistant, Bruce Piersawl, check the manuscript's length. Although the contract calls for no more than 100,000 words, in my eagerness to have it live up to the adjective in its title I have written 125,000. The manuscript will have to be cut, Fox says, lest the book be too bulky and thus more expensive than the market will bear.

I sharpen some pencils and start trimming. I easily find unneeded phrases here and there, as well as an occasional paragraph that will not, I reluctantly concede, be missed. At the same time I think of a number of additional facts and anecdotes that will, it seems to me, improve the manuscript. Against my will, and certainly against Fox's, it grows.

I drop it off at Random House again. The next morning, uncharacteristically early, Fox telephones. I have cut the manuscript, he informs me with ill-disguised exasperation, from 125,000 to 130,000 words. Sheepishly, I tell him I did my best. Fox, a man well schooled in the irrationalities of authors, says he gives up. He will go ahead and publish the book at the length I have so defiantly written it.

As Fox predicted, the size of *The Complete Book of Running*—it is 320 pages long and packaged in a larger than usual format—presents a problem. When the costs of typesetting, paper and binding are calculated, it turns out that according to the formulas customarily employed, it should sell for $12.95 or more. However, Random House's marketing experts feel that at this price it might be too expensive for its intended audience; before I turned in the manuscript at such inordinate length they had hoped to price it at no more than $10.00. Now, weighing probable sales, they decide to take a risk and charge $10.00 anyway. With any luck, enough additional readers may buy the book to make up for the lower profit margin.*

April 4

Joe Fox tells me it is time to think about a jacket for *The Complete Book of Running.* Could I drop by and talk it over?

---

*When the book finally goes on sale, a number of readers and reviewers remark that for its size it is a bargain. Quality aside, they are quite right.

April 11

I go to Fox's office, which is on the eleventh floor of
a building on East 50th Street. He introduces me to
Bob Scudellari, Random House's chief art director,
and a talented young designer who will be responsible
for my book. Fox tells me it was Scudellari who devised the successful jacket for Timothy Gallwey's *The
Inner Game of Tennis*—a lush tennis ball so lovingly
illuminated and photographed that the viewer could
practically smell its hermetic brand-newness. Then,
sitting down, Fox vanishes behind a yellowing pillar
of newspapers that for no discernible reason perpetu-
ally occupies the northeast quadrant of his desk. (Seeing it for the first time, I remember thinking of my Boy
Scout scrap-collecting efforts during World War II
and wondering if perhaps Fox, having similarly taken
up the practice at that time, had enjoyed himself so
much that he could never bring himself to abandon
it.)

Scudellari, who is tall, bright-eyed and irrepressibly
enthusiastic, asks whether I have any ideas for the
jacket. Standing up, I demonstrate my only suggestion: a runner, arms outstretched in triumph, crossing
a finish line.

Joe, observing, peers around his newsprint barri-
cade. Scudellari, the designer and he exchange politely
silent frowns. I sense that I have not solved their
problem.

Scudellari, seizing a pencil and a scrap of paper,
sketches. "What if," he asks, "we were to photograph
a pair of running legs against a red background?" The
results, he says, could be every bit as striking as the
Gallwey tennis ball.

He even has a photographer in mind, he says—Neal
Slavin, the same person who photographed the cele-

brated tennis ball. Could I come to Slavin's studio sometime the following week and bring some red running clothes? When the time comes to make the actual jacket photograph, Scudellari explains, a professional model will, needless to say, be hired. My presence now, however, will permit Slavin to experiment at leisure in order to discover how to photograph the legs in the most effective way.

The Boston Marathon is scheduled for next Monday—twenty-six miles that can transform a sane man or woman into a whimpering, exhausted neurotic. I tell Scudellari that if no disaster befalls me in Boston I will be at Slavin's studio at the specified time.

April 20

Having run one of my fastest marathons at Boston day before yesterday, I am creaky. When I grit my teeth and try diligently, however, I am nonetheless able to run. I pack a pair of red nylon running shorts and some red shoes. With my son John along for company, I go to Slavin's studio, a refitted loft in downtown Manhattan. Scudellari, looking cheerful and eager to get started, is already there.

Slavin, a quiet, bearded man of Talmudic meditativeness, has had two young assistants build a forty-foot running track out of plywood and tubular-steel construction scaffolding. It is elevated some four feet off the floor in order, as Slavin explains it, to allow him to place his four-by-five view camera precisely at ground level.

"So far as I know," he says, "no one else has made this kind of photograph, so at least we'll start off with that advantage."

I dress in my running clothes and, when Slavin tells me to, climb onto the track. Looking through a viewfinder, Slavin instructs me to try running. Tentatively, I do so. The elevated plywood sags and creaks ominously wherever it is not directly supported by scaffolding. I kneel and take a close look at it. It is three-eighths of an inch thick. I would feel only slightly more secure if twice that thickness were under me.

"Again. Faster this time," Slavin calls out.

Nervously, I mention my anxieties about the plywood. I imagine myself plummeting, not unlike a wrecking ball, through the sagging plywood and the floor underneath it and into the loft below Slavin's.

"Don't worry about it," Slavin says cheerfully. "It's plenty strong. I tested it myself. Faster!"

I follow his instructions. Slavin's strobe lights pop and flash. The plywood bends under me. Scudellari studies a polaroid Slavin has made. Lights are shifted for better effect.

A sheet of heavy red paper, as broad as a living room carpet, is unfurled from a roller above the track. It is the photograph's intended background. Slavin makes a pencil mark on the paper where it curls onto the plywood track. My left foot, he says, must be precisely on the mark each time a photograph is made.

By practicing, I soon learn to hit the mark whenever I want to. Slavin takes several more polaroids. We look at them. My legs look terrible. Under Slavin's artful side lighting the muscles have a nicely sculptured definition, but the skin looks so pale it might belong to a Welsh miner. Furthermore, far from giving the desired impression of boundlessly joyous energy, my red running shoes appear scarcely to leave the ground; for all a viewer would know, their soles might have sprouted roots.

Slavin sends one of his assistants to a drugstore to buy some Man Tan. I rub it on, from thigh to ankle.

Slavin and Scudellari watch approvingly as I darken. Soon my legs are burnished like well-weathered pine. Continuing to make tests, Slavin takes some more polaroids. We look at them. Although nicely basted now, my legs still lack energy. Slavin tells me to try to lift my knees higher. I do so. The results, although more satisfactory, are not what he is hoping for.

"We've got to do something about this," he muses unhappily.

As an experiment, I try running with an exaggerated prance, much as an overconscientious drum majorette might. It would, I estimate, take me half a day and not a few charley horses to finish even a short race using such a gait, but mysteriously this improbable motion looks exactly right when it is photographed.

Slavin and Scudellari confer. Slavin tells me, "Let's try a few more, with Ektachrome this time. These polaroids are looking pretty good now. Who knows? We may not need to hire a model after all."

I run a dozen more times, hitting the mark with practiced precision each time. Finally Slavin and Scudellari declare themselves satisfied. As for me, I am worn out. First the Boston Marathon and then a day on the world's most perilously rickety running track are enough for a single week.

April 22

Joe Fox telephones. He has seen Neal Slavin's photographs and is delighted. A mockup of the jacket, incorporating both a photograph and the required type, will now be prepared and, a few days later, shown to the Random House sales force at their semiannual sales conference for their reactions. This, however, is a mere formality, Fox assures me; they are certain to love it.

April 28–May 13

Fox phones again. To his and Scudellari's considerable surprise, the jacket was not at all well received. The sales force felt the legs were too obviously those of an experienced runner and would therefore put off the ordinary jogger. Furthermore, women readers, several of those present insisted, would never accept a book that bore only a man's legs; there should be a woman's legs on the jacket as well. Since women buy so many of the books published in the United States, this reservation must be allowed to prevail.

An alternative jacket is prepared. Bob Handville, the artist whose illustrations will appear throughout the interior of the book, is asked to render several running figures—a child, an elderly woman, an overweight man, a trim college athlete. These, intended to suggest running's wide appeal, are then scattered over a yellow background.

Handville's drawings are fine, but the overall effect is awful; the jacket is neither coherent nor, everyone who sees it agrees, inviting. Unfortunately, if the book is to meet its schedule there is no time to do a third jacket. Random House therefore abandons Jacket No. 2 and puts its hope, none too confidently, in the photograph of my ridiculously prancing, Man Tanned legs.*

May 5

The editorial and sales executives at Random House are trying to make up their minds. Shall they print 12,500 copies of *The Complete Book of Running* or, more optimistically, 15,000? It is not an easy question.

*In publishing, paradoxes abound. It will quickly become clear, once the book goes on sale, that the jacket alone, at one time considered so dangerously problematical, is responsible for much of its success.

True, it is clear that there seem to be more runners around than there were, but how many more? And will an appreciable number buy copies of the book?

Finally Tony Schulte ends the discussion with a surprising proposal. "Let's go with twenty-five thousand," he says. "I can't step out my front door these days without being knocked down by a jogger."

A salesman who is present shakes his head doubtfully. He is not at all sure, he says, that he and his colleagues can obtain orders for that many copies of a book on a subject as obscure as running still is.

Not long afterward the *New York Times Sunday Magazine,* a publication that keeps a sharp eye out for current trends, publishes a cover story on jogging; the sport's extraordinary growth and future prospects are documented at length. Almost immediately the flow of orders from bookstores picks up. Random House raises its print order to 35,000 copies.

May 9

Julian Bach telephones me with cheerful concern. "You had better get in touch with your accountant right away," he says. "If the first printing sells out, even though the book does nothing more than that, you're going to have a lot of money coming in. Unless you do something about it, the IRS is going to grab half of it right off the bat."

After Bach hangs up I do some calculating. Under my contract I receive 10 percent of the book's $10 retail price on the first 7,500 copies. That comes to $7,500. Thereafter Random House pays me 12½ percent on the next 2,500 copies, or $3,125, and 15 percent beyond that. Thus the first printing alone, should it sell in its entirety, would earn me $48,125. Out of that would come the $10,000 Random House has advanced me. Ten percent of the rest, or $3,812, would go to Bach. I would be left with $34,313.

I am too embarrassed to tell my agent that I do not even know an accountant, let alone have one. Nor do I let him know, for fear of seeming as naive about money as I know myself to be, that I can't bring myself to worry much about the possibility that the Internal Revenue Service will take its rightful share of more money than I have ever, in my forty-five years, possessed at one time.

May 15–June 3

An author need not always wait until his book is published to get at least a rough-and-ready idea of what readers are likely to think of it. There exists, in fact, an elaborate and generally quite accurate early-warning system.

One element of this system consists of sales to magazines. Partly for publicity and partly to earn fees that may range from a few hundred to several thousand dollars, prepublication excerpts are typically offered to various publications well before a book's release date. If interest is brisk, it is taken as a promising sign.

As soon as my manuscript has been Xeroxed, therefore, Julian Bach sends chapters to *Reader's Digest, Sports Illustrated, Playboy, Esquire, McCall's, Redbook* and *Family Health.* The apathy is ominous. Not one of them wants to publish any of the book, and several editors go out of their way to tell Bach, by way of friendly explanation, that their readers have no interest in running.

Finally, however, some good news arrives. The *Ladies' Home Journal* takes a small excerpt, a chapter on running for women, and pays $750 for it. Because it is intended only for a single regional edition of the magazine rather than for the entire press run, however, the sale does little to enhance anyone's optimism.

June 8

The Book-of-the-Month Club, shown *The Complete Book of Running* as soon as galley proofs are available, outbids the Literary Guild for book-club rights, paying $28,000. Half goes to Random House and 10 percent of the remainder to Julian Bach. That leaves me $12,600. Best of all, it costs me nothing in either time or effort. I am beginning to find this an uncommonly congenial way to earn a living.

June 10

I mention the Book-of-the-Month Club sale to a young editor friend, Martha Oestreicher. She exclaims, "Gee, Jim, it looks as if you're going to have a best seller."

"Impossible," I tell her. "Sports books don't make best sellers."

I mean it. I have, in fact, long since started writing a modest children's book in hopes of augmenting my income once *The Complete Book of Running* has stopped selling. After all, there is no point in going back to magazine work any sooner than I have to.

July 5–19

Even though a professional indexer would charge only $500 or so to prepare an index for *The Complete Book of Running,* I spend two weeks compulsively doing it myself (and in the process practically smothering in three-by-five cards). When I tell a friend, Charles Steinmetz, how I am spending my time, he laughs and refers me to Kurt Vonnegut's novel *Cat's Cradle.* There, I discover, Vonnegut writes that "indexing was a thing that only the most amateurish author undertook to do for his own book."

I start to worry. Vonnegut may be right.

October 23

Publication day at last! Not in any particular spirit of exultation or celebration but simply because nothing else needs to be done, I compete in the New York City Marathon. Waiting for the start at Fort Wadsworth on Staten Island, I see a runner reading the Sunday *Times.* I borrow the book review section. Random House has placed a full-page advertisement for my book. I read it. It says, "The freshness and *joie de vivre* that James Fixx brings to *The Complete Book of Running* is extraordinary in itself. His special love for running is as infectious as the sound of a packed stadium cheering." Tears come to my eyes.

The 1977 New York City Marathon turns out to be my worst performance in five years. There is, I discover, nothing like the sedentary labor of writing a running book to play hell with one's own running. Three or four hundred consecutive days seated at a desk, even when leavened by a daily hour or so on the roads, does little to augment one's cardiovascular fitness. For the entire twenty-six miles I feel sluggish. The doughnut of flab that has congealed around my midsection is, I suspect, partly responsible.

There is, on the other hand, one hopeful augury. Alice, waiting for me at the finish line, notices a woman in the crowd. She is carrying a copy of *The Complete Book of Running.* The book has been out less than half a day.

October 24–30

The day after the marathon, Random House permits me twenty-four hours to recover. Thereupon I am dispatched on a book-promotion tour that has been devised with such tireless diligence that there is seldom time in my schedule for anything but airports, television studios and the small, airless rooms newspapers set aside for the purpose, I come to suspect, of shortening interviews with visiting publicity seekers like me.

On the *Today* show, early in the tour, I encounter Michael Korda, who is traveling the country in an effort to enhance sales of *Power!,* his sequel to his best-selling nonfiction work *Success!* Korda, a publisher himself and an old hand at publicizing books, offers me a veteran's advice.

"When you start out on one of these trips," he says, "be sure you have everything you need. If you have to go out and buy so much as a toothbrush, it can throw a whole day's schedule out of kilter."

I take Korda's observation as a joke. Before many days have passed, however, I realize he was entirely in earnest.

I am scheduled to visit ten cities, from Washington and Boston to Los Angeles and San Francisco, in as many working days. My itinerary for Minneapolis and St. Paul is exhaustingly typical:

9:00 A.M. "Twin Cities Today," KSTP-TV
10:30 A.M. "Boone & Ericson," WCCO radio
12 noon "Midday," WCCO-TV
1:30 P.M. "News and Views," KMSP-TV
2:30 P.M. *St. Paul Press/Dispatch*
3:45 P.M. *Minneapolis Tribune*

After that, there's a hurried taxi to the airport and, at night, another hotel room in another city.

At the end of such a day, much as one may crave respite, one cannot invariably count on any. En route to Dallas, my plane is delayed by weather. When I finally arrive at my hotel it is two o'clock in the morning. A bellhop takes me upstairs. I tip him and say goodnight.

Puzzling over my name on the slip of paper in his hand, he looks at me and asks, "You aren't the fellow who wrote that running book, are you?"

I acknowledge that I am.

"I do a little running myself," he tells me.

Although it is several hours past my bedtime, I try to express appropriate pleasure at the news.

"Unfortunately," he goes on, "two or three weeks ago I injured my foot—a stress fracture, I think. Here, take a look."

Seating himself on the bed, he removes his shoe and sock. "Put your hand there," he instructs me.

By the time he has finally laced his shoe back on I am feeling murderous. The fortunate bellhop little suspects how close he has come to breathing his last right there in my hotel room.

On the other hand, touring does have its frequent pleasures. In Cleveland I encounter Fred Griffith, a runner himself and the host of a popular television program, *The Morning Exchange,* and we become friends. In Minneapolis I meet an imaginative *Tribune* columnist, Larry Batson, whose friendship and graceful essays enormously enrich my life. And in Portland I come across Oz Hopkins, a feature writer for the *Oregonian,* for whom I develop an immediate and lasting affection. There are others, too.

Interviewers, I discover, vary greatly. Some seem abidingly interested in their subjects, others mostly in getting a job done with as little effort as possible. On the *Today* show I am interviewed by the co-host, Tom Brokaw. He and I are seated side by side, three cameras facing us. His voice and expression radiating sincerity, he asks me a question. As I start to answer he turns away and—the live camera is on me alone now —begins gesticulating to a colleague. I find myself addressing my reply to Brokaw's right sideburn. For a novice at television, talking to a man who clearly isn't listening is an unnerving experience.

In Boston, Random House provides me with a chauffeur-driven limousine, only the second one, so far as I can remember, in which I have ever ridden. (The first was back in 1950, on the day my father died.) The car is so startlingly elongated that from the back seat I have to squint to see its distant prow. While we are stopped for a traffic light, two high school girls walk by. Looking into the car and seeing me, one exclaims, "Don't you got the life!"

As my tour continues, I come to see that many if not most people riding in chauffeured limousines are, sad to say, not going anywhere they would choose to go if they had anything to say about it. I even think of a title for a book on the drawbacks of being a celebrity: *The Trouble with Limousines.*

October 31

One of the first celebrities I encounter on my publicity tour, as well as one of the most genuine and generous, is Gavin McLeod. He and I meet on a Washington, D.C., talk show, *Panorama*. McLeod has long been applauded for his portrayal of Murray, the newswriter, on *The Mary Tyler Moore Show*, and he will soon assume the starring role in *The Love Boat*. I, by contrast, am the unknown author of an almost unknown book.

McLeod and I, seated on a couch with the show's host, are introduced. I am asked two or three questions. Thereupon, attention shifts to McLeod and his television adventures—and stays there. Because time is running out, it seems unlikely that the *Panorama* audience will hear any more about me or *The Complete Book of Running* that I am seeking so diligently to publicize.

The typical celebrity thrives on massive doses of attention. Curiously, however, as the minutes go by I notice that McLeod is becoming increasingly restive in the limelight. Finally, interrupting the host in mid-sentence, he picks up a copy of my book, holds the jacket squarely up to one of the cameras, and says to me, "But what I'm really interested in, Jim, is how you got the idea for a book on running."

Plainly, his discomfort had been the result of his awareness that I was being neglected. I could have kissed him.

November 2

I am scheduled to appear on *A.M. Chicago,* a popular talk show. I am in the green room. Michael Korda and Gunther Gebel-Williams, the wild-animal trainer, are here, too. I have been touring for more than a week and am exhausted. Gebel-Williams, publicizing a forthcoming appearance with the Ringling circus, is being interviewed. I watch him on a monitor. I am scheduled to go on next, after a commercial.

Waiting to be called, I find myself feeling strangely anxious and disoriented. I do not understand why.

An aide comes to the green room and escorts me to the studio. I am told to sit in a high director's chair. A technician clips a microphone to my necktie. Inexplicably, I feel dizzy, as if I might fall out of the chair. My hands are trembling and my palms are wet.

The commercial is on. My interviewer, smiling, sits down beside me and reviews some notes in her lap. A red light above a camera lens comes on, indicating

that this is the camera whose image the audience is
seeing.

The woman introduces me and holds my book up
to the camera, its jacket tilted downward to avoid
reflections from the overhead lights. She asks me a
friendly question. As if from a great distance I hear
myself replying. I feel faint. My heart is beating so
hard that I fear the microphone must be picking up its
hammering.

I realize I cannot go on with the interview.

"I'm not feeling well," I say. I am weak and nearly
overcome with vertigo.

My interviewer looks at me, plainly wondering
whether I am joking. Seeing that I am not, she quickly
terminates our conversation. The red light on the camera facing me goes out. Hurriedly, another commercial is shown.

Taking me by the arm, someone leads me from the
set. Several members of the *A.M. Chicago* staff gather
around me, concerned. At once, except for my embarrassment, which is acute, I feel better. My hands are
no longer trembling. My heart does not pound. Soon
I am left only with a puzzlement about what happened. Was I sick or what? Here I am, trying to publicize a book on physical fitness, and I've just fallen
apart in front of one of the Midwest's biggest television audiences.

Joe Fox telephones me at my hotel. He is worried. He
tells me that Michael Korda, whose book is also published by Random House, called him in alarm after
my collapse.

"What in the world happened?" Fox asks me.

"I guess I was just worn out," I tell him.

Somehow I know, however, that whatever occurred
is more complicated than that.

November 3–4

The telephone rings. It is a woman from the Public Broadcasting System's *MacNeil-Lehrer Report.* They plan to air a program the following evening on the significance of the running phenomenon and wonder whether I am available to be part of their panel of experts. Having had one disastrous television experience, I am not eager to do the show. Still, it is an important one. Nervously I fly to New York, take a Valium provided by a solicitous friend, and, thus benumbed, manage to get through the program without another collapse.

As I search for the cause of my nervousness, I realize something odd. I now feel panicky not just about television appearances—a comfortably limited problem, after all—but about public appearances in general, including speeches. Unaccountably, my malady is spreading, as if it were not a psychological disorder at all but poison ivy.

November 7

Perhaps, a friend suggests, I have somehow developed a phobia. The hypothesis, I am startled to realize, is not implausible. Physically I feel excellent. As usual, I am running ten miles a day and sometimes more. I sleep well. My appetite is good. So far as I can see, it is only when I am in front of a television camera or an audience that I am troubled by my baffling anxieties.

In ordinary circumstances the problem would be little cause for worry. After all, most of us are rarely required to appear on television or make a speech, nor are our lives demonstrably poorer for our obscurity.

My case, however, is different. I am in the middle of that sine qua non of successful book promotion, the author tour. Both my publisher and Alice have assured me that it is a rare book these days that sells well without such an effort. If *The Complete Book of Running* is to have any chance of enjoying a good sale, there is no turning back.

Anxious to find a solution, I telephone a friend who is a doctor. He confirms the first friend's hypothesis.

"What's happened to you is common," he says. "It sounds like a classic phobia. Plenty of actors and public speakers, even seasoned professionals, have them. You'd be surprised how many great performances have begun with an actor or actress throwing up backstage. Furthermore, phobias characteristically come on without any warning, exactly as yours did."

He explains that there are two principal ways of dealing with a phobia. The sufferer can enter into psychotherapy in hopes of laboriously searching out the problem's causes; such a process can take months, or in some cases years, and can cost large amounts of money. Or he can undertake a supervised course of behavior modification that, if successful, breaks the panic pattern without necessarily revealing what caused it.

My friend tells me about a phobia clinic that has recently been established at a hospital in White Plains, New York, not far from my home.

"It's just the thing for people like you," he says cheerfully. "It will turn your neurotic anxieties into everyday terrors."

I telephone the hospital. A woman with an English accent and a reassuring manner tells me the clinic meets once a week. She invites me to sit in on the next session. Fortunately, I am free for a few days before my publicity tour resumes, so I am able to tell her I will be happy to accept her invitation.

November 9

Arriving at the clinic, I find a dozen or so people, all of them women, seated at a round table in a pleasant, sunny room. They look alert, friendly and as disarmingly normal as the members of a great books discussion group. One of the women introduces herself as Melanie Sharp-Bolster, the leader.

The session begins. Mrs. Sharp-Bolster invites comments from the group. One woman, who says she becomes fearful whenever she is required to venture outside her house, reports that she recently completed a trip to the A&P without mishap. Mrs. Sharp-Bolster congratulates her. Another, who says she feels panicky whenever she is behind the wheel of her automobile, reports that although she has not yet succeeded in bringing herself to drive, she is now able to sit in the driver's seat even when the engine is running. Mrs. Sharp-Bolster, telling her it is a promising improvement, urges her to keep trying. A third woman, who appears to be nineteen or twenty years old, discusses a long-standing fear of having her food poisoned and says her anxiety prevents her from accepting dinner dates or visiting friends' homes for meals.

"The only food I'm able to eat," she tells the group, "is what I prepare for myself." Her phobia, she explains, is a considerable inconvenience. Thus she is eager, if possible, to find a way to rid herself of it.

A member of the group makes a suggestion. "Could you," she asks, "buy some groceries yourself and then have a friend you trust cook a meal for you while you supervise its preparation?"

"Yes," the young woman replies. "I suppose I wouldn't be particularly fearful of that."

"Next," the other woman goes on, "you could buy your own groceries, as before, but have your friend cook the meal while you weren't present. If you took the process in small steps, you might be able to overcome your phobia after a while."

An expression of amused long-suffering comes over the young woman's face.

"I don't think you quite understand," she says. "What you're suggesting is a *rational* solution. My phobia is *irrational.*"

Finally Mrs. Sharp-Bolster invites me to speak. I describe the *A.M. Chicago* incident and my puzzlement over it. I am, I say, much like the young woman with the food phobia. Rationally, I am not fearful of television cameras or audiences, nor am I apprehensive about being embarrassed or caught without an answer. Ever since Chicago, the camera and I have simply had a wretchedly uneasy relationship, and the same has mysteriously been true of live audiences.

Mrs. Sharp-Bolster makes a suggestion. "Sometimes," she says, "phobias diminish in time if you repeatedly expose yourself to their causes. As you become convinced that television doesn't constitute a real danger, your anxiety should lessen and eventually disappear. The key is to expose yourself to what you fear in small, nonthreatening doses."

Exposing myself to television, I reflect unhappily, is what I've got to do anyway if I'm going to publicize my book the way everyone insists I must. Besides, how would I possibly arrange for a small, nonthreatening dose of David Hartman or Tom Brokaw? No, it's either all or nothing.

As politely as I can, I thank Mrs. Sharp-Bolster for

her suggestion. It is the last time I visit the phobia clinic. I am, it seems, on my own.

November 10

Random House sends me some early reviews of my book. Out-of-town reviewers are almost uniformly generous in their praise, but some of the major ones, those who write for the important magazines and newspapers, are far from kind. In the *New York Times* Christopher Lehmann-Haupt writes of the book, "The essential information it contains could probably have been squeezed into a pamphlet." *Sports Illustrated* headlines its review "The Joy of Running Comes Through, But, Oh, How the Author Runs On." (Could it be those added 5,000 words?) *Time* hasn't mentioned it, nor has *Newsweek.* Maybe it's just as well.

Several reviewers, I notice, remark on how complete the index is. Nonetheless, I cautiously keep it a secret that it is home-made.

November 13

Although I have long since left the Midwest, the *A.M. Chicago* incident continues to trouble me. My concern arises not only from my bafflement over exactly what happened. There is no way, it seems clear, that my collapse could have failed to hurt sales of the book wherever the program is seen. Yet today, on the *Chicago Tribune*'s best-seller list, a new title appears. I can't believe it, but there it is: *The Complete Book of Running.*

November 15

I am waiting, having dosed myself with Valium, to appear on a talk show, *Denver Now.* An old family friend, Patty Hodgins, has come to the studio; afterward she and I plan to have dinner at the Brown Palace.

"Are you getting tired of these interviews?" Patty asks me. I have, as she knows, been at it for three full weeks.

"They're not usually too tedious," I tell her. "I try to treat each one as if it were the first interview I've ever done. It's only when I have to answer a really familiar question that it gets tiresome."

"What's the most familiar question you hear?" Patty asks me.

I tell her, "I guess it's 'If I've never run before, what would you recommend that I do to get started?' "

The interview begins. The show's host, Beverly Martinez, smiles winningly, introduces me, displays the jacket of my book and asks, "Jim, suppose a person has never run before. How should he or she get started?"

November 18

There is, I am coming to feel, a fundamental contradiction in setting forth to publicize a book. Most of us are taught that it is proper to be self-effacing and modest, yet in traveling the country on a publicity tour we must contrive to be exactly the opposite, or our time—along with the publisher's money—is wasted. The task either becomes an increasingly vexatious struggle against one's best instincts, or else one simply ceases struggling and turns into an insensitive, publicity-seeking egomaniac. Today in mid-interview, with the television cameras directed at me, I found myself wondering: *What in the world are you doing here, Fixx?*

November 21

I am in San Francisco, the last city on this part of the
tour. I take a taxi across the Bay Bridge to the office
of the *Oakland Tribune.* As I wait in the lobby to talk
with Andy Morgensen, the reporter assigned to interview me, another reporter comes through the city
room door. He holds a copy of *The Complete Book of
Running.*

"I think your book is terrific," he says. "Would you
autograph it for me?"

His request startles me. It is one of the few times
anyone has asked for my autograph, and the very first
time since *The Complete Book of Running* was published. It seems niggardly to sign only my name, so I
write above it, "Run!"

Uninspired as the injunction is, the reporter, reading it, looks thoroughly satisfied.

November 23

I am resting in my room at the Stanford Court Hotel
on Nob Hill, trying to gather nerve and momentum
for my next interview. The telephone rings.

"Mr. Fixx?" a voice inquires. "This is Bob Boyle at
Sports Illustrated. We're planning to run a 'Scorecard'
item on this big best seller you've written."

"Big best seller?" I ask. I have had no idea it was
doing well enough for *Sports Illustrated* to take an
interest in it.

"It certainly is," says Boyle. "Your publisher took
in orders for eighty-five thousand copies during the
first week alone, and they keep coming in faster than
he can count them. The printer can't get them off the
press fast enough."

When at last Boyle and I finish our conversation I

sit down, put my face in my hands and, unable to help myself, cry. For nearly two years I have worked on *The Complete Book of Running* without any idea of what its reception might be. Now, at last, I know.

I am aware that a new phase of my life is beginning —and not only because, within five days of publication, I earned, if Boyle is right, $114,750.

III

"I Have Some Good News and Some Bad News"

November 24

Julian Bach telephones. "There's nothing but excellent news," he says. Sales, he tells me, are uniformly strong and the reviews, coming in from around the country, are increasingly favorable. Perhaps most pleasing of all, the book will soon appear on, of all places, the *New York Times* best-seller list.

I can't believe it. Seeing my name on the *Chicago Tribune* list was exciting enough, but this is the big leagues. No doubt about it now, I'm a bona fide best-selling author.

November 25

Bach telephones again. Even though the first royalty payments are not due until next summer, Random House has offered to release some money now in order to help spread my income out. Royalties right away, Bach explains, would let the payments fall into two years instead of only one and might thus lower the taxes I will have to pay.

"The book is selling so strongly," Bach says, "that you're going to have a much more serious problem than we thought."

I ask how large a payment Random House is proposing.

"Fifty thousand dollars would present no difficulties at all," he says.

November 27

The Complete Book of Running appears, for the first time, on the *Times* best-seller list. It is in the No. 12 position in the nonfiction category—not very high, to be sure, but nicely anchored all the same. At a neighborhood dinner party I meet a young woman. She says, "I've never met a best-selling author before. May I touch you?"

With a forefinger she touches me lightly on the lapel, smiling contentedly as she does so.

November 28

I receive a call from a pleasant-sounding man who tells me his name is Roy Fields. Fields informs me that he serves as a distributor for a firm that sells bottles containing bee-pollen tablets ("the forgotten wonder food"). He asks if I, as an increasingly well-known sports figure and author, might be interested in endorsing his pollen, which is imported from France and is said to bring dramatic improvements in athletic performance. By messenger, he sends me 250 pale brown tablets and some promotional literature:

> Ambrosia. To the ancients from the Norseland to Mount Olympus, it was the food of the gods and believed to insure eternal life. . . . Evidence today points toward its contents. In all likelihood, ambrosia was a bittersweet combination of honey and "bee bread." Or, in other words, bee pollen.

I promise Fields I will try the tablets. Who knows? Maybe they will improve my running.

December 1

A friendly and enthusiastic Charlotte, North Carolina, department-store executive, Ervin Jackson of the Ivey's chain, writes to invite me to visit some of his stores and autograph books on the Saturday before an important local race, the Charlotte Observer Marathon. "The magic of your presence," he tells me in his letter, "would magnify the marathon as well as your book."

December 4

The book climbs to No. 5 on the *Times* best-seller list. Clearly hoping to shield me from disappointment, my son John comments, "Dad, if I were you I wouldn't count on its going any higher than that."

I am touched by his concern.

Then, reflectively, John adds, "Come to think of it, I'm not sure a book like yours belongs even that high."

He may be right.

December 15–18

With John I fly to Charlotte in hopes of effecting the magnifications so confidently predicted by Ervin Jackson. So far as I can determine, however, the only thing that is noticeably larger than life in Charlotte that weekend is Jackson's irrepressible prose style.

December 19

An upsetting letter arrives at Random House. It is from a California publisher named Bob Anderson. The founder of a magazine called *Runner's World,* Anderson demands either that my book be withdrawn from the market or that Random House pay a fee to his firm.

In large part because of the skillful efforts of its editor, a gifted young journalist-athlete named Joe Henderson, Anderson's publication is the most widely read periodical on running, and he issues occasional books and pamphlets on the sport as well. Declaring himself "incensed," he points out that in several passages in *The Complete Book of Running* I have quoted from *Runner's World.*

Anderson's letter astonishes me. Most of the references to his magazine are in a chapter subtitled "The Runner's Own Cult Magazine." In it, on the basis of interviews with him and with Henderson as well as on years of familiarity with the magazine, I describe *Runner's World* as the "best and most influential running publication ever devised by the mind of man." I had supposed that Anderson would be pleased.

A Random House lawyer will reply to the letter in an effort to head off trouble.

December 20

The book has been in stores a little more than a month; 155,000 copies have been sold. The telephone rings. It is a reporter for *People,* Mary Vespa.

"We want to do a story on you and your best seller," she says. "I've lined up a photographer. We hope to come out and spend a few hours with you week after next."

I tell her to come ahead. It's not every day, after all, that a magazine like *People* takes an interest in a quite ordinary person like me.

"Just plan to spend the day exactly as you usually would," she says. "We want you to be completely natural."

December 22

A check for $45,000 arrives—the $50,000 Julian Bach mentioned, less his 10 percent commission. I stop in at the local bank to deposit it. The teller, a pretty woman in her twenties, seems unsurprised by the amount, handling the transaction with cool efficiency. At length, however, her reserve crumbles. Handing me a receipt, she smiles brightly and asks, "Are you married?"

January 2, 1978

Miss Vespa, who is dark-haired and pretty and radiates sincerity, arrives with a bearded, intense photographer named Ken Regan, who is most widely known for playfully clicking his heels as the golfer Ben Crenshaw takes his picture in a Canon camera commercial. At their request I have, with no little difficulty, assembled the entire family—Alice, my eldest sons Paul and John, and the twins, Betsy and Stephen. Our faces are nicely scrubbed and our hair is combed. We all want to look our best.

While Regan unpacks his Nikons—not Canons!—and enough Tri-X film to assure Kodak a banner year, Miss Vespa draws me aside for the first of several interrogations that will take place throughout the long day we spend together. "How much do you weigh?" she asks, scrutinizing me.

"On a good day, a hundred and fifty-five pounds," I tell her.

"What did you weigh before you took up running?"

"Two hundred and twenty pounds. I looked like a prize pig."

"How much have you earned from your book?"

"Two hundred thousand dollars by this time."

Stephen, who is a silent, macho fourteen years old, wanders toward the refrigerator, foraging for something to eat. Miss Vespa asks, "Do you jog, Steve?"

Without breaking stride Stephen replies, "Jogging is boring."

Miss Vespa has hit pay dirt and knows it. She writes Stephen's comment in her notebook.

Regan says he is ready for me. "Just be completely natural," he instructs me. "I want you sitting here on your basement steps, surrounded by your running shoes and drinking this can of beer."

He pops the top and hands the can to me.

I tell Regan that I seldom if ever sit on my basement steps, nor do I characteristically drink beer in the basement, particularly at this hour of the morning.

Regan overrules my objections. "This is going to be a dynamite picture," he says. "Just sit on this step, enjoy the beer and look completely natural."

Reluctant to diminish his buoyant enthusiasm, I sit down where he tells me to. He shoots several rolls of film, smiling devilishly.

January 16–23

People appears on newstands. The basement photograph is, of course, the one that leads the story. Furthermore, sitting there on the steps, a Budweiser in my hand and a relaxed smile on my face, I do, I have to admit, look completely natural.

As for Miss Vespa's text, Stephen's iconoclastic comment finds its way into a caption, while an early para-graph gives prominent attention to the $200,000 I have earned. A few days later, thieves break into our house and make off with jewelry, silverware, two 35-millimeter cameras and a television set.

The *People* story produces a happier sequel as well. I receive a letter from a woman in Connecticut who identifies herself as a former first-grade classmate for whom, when we were six years old, I had a vast, if not exactly requited, passion. Reading the magazine, she tells me, she was struck by seeing my name but was not certain at first that the Jim Fixx in the story was the same Jim Fixx she had known four decades earlier.

"Then," she writes, "I looked at the eyes in the photograph and, sure enough, they were your eyes."

January 24–February 2

An unsettling exchange of correspondence between Bob Anderson's attorney and the Random House law-yer develops, petering out only after I produce a letter from Henderson in which he has written, "Naturally you have permission to use anything you like from *Runner's World.* Among other things, we can't get this kind of free publicity many places!" As my first experience of this kind, however, it has been worri-some.*

---

*The *Runner's World* incident will ultimately have two aftereffects. The first is that Henderson, a respected editor and writer and the author of several books about running, leaves his post at *Runner's World* to join a rival magazine. He tells me that Anderson's rancor over his public praise of my book, which by this time constitutes at least modest competition for his own publications, was a factor.

The second occurs when Anderson, having come east on business, invites me to lunch at his hotel, the St. Regis. Over our coffee, Anderson, who since I interviewed him in California has cultivated a luxuriant beard, says, "There's something I want to bring up. It's about our recent ex-change of letters. Do you understand what I'm referring to?"

I tell him I think I do.

February 3

A nineteen-year-old aspiring actress writes me from Pasadena, California. Concerned because she has recently gained thirty pounds, she asks, "If I were to come to Connecticut would you help me in my training? Losing weight is only the first step. I would then like to condition every muscle in my body and one day run in the Boston Marathon. I would also love to train for the Olympics."

As gently as I can, I tell her no.

February 4

Julian Bach telephones. An Australian firm, Outback Press, has asked about acquiring rights to publish and sell my book in Australia and New Zealand.

"They've offered an advance of three thousand dollars," he says, "but I've managed to work them up to four thousand. If it sounds all right to you I'll go ahead with the contract."

I tell him it sounds fine. I can't think of many easier ways to earn $4,000.*

"If you had come to me," he goes on, "and had told me you wanted to concentrate on Henderson instead of on me, I would have said fine. What bothered me was not even being asked."

Now I understand the cause of Anderson's distress. I remember a winter afternoon while I was writing the book. I had mailed Henderson a draft of my chapter on *Runner's World,* asking him to call any errors to my attention. To my surprise, it was Anderson rather than Henderson who telephoned. For an hour or more, clearly disturbed by the attention I had given Henderson, he enumerated his own contributions to the magazine and to the world of running, urging me to take notes as he spoke.

The source of much of the difficulty, it is now plain, has been that I simply hurt Anderson's feelings. I wonder how many lawsuits are instigated for no more substantial reason than that.

*In the following months Bach will sell rights in some fifteen countries. Chatto & Windus in London pays $6,200, Editions Robert Laffont in Paris $18,400, Editorial Atlantida in Buenos Aires $10,500, and rights are sold for lesser amounts in Italy, Japan, Brazil, Israel, Greece and each of the

February 5

No. 2 in the *Times!* Only James Herriot's *All Things Wise and Wonderful* stands between my book and the very top of the best-seller list. My mother mails me a silver charm. On it she has had engraved the date and "No. 2." She has a gift for understatement; this is about as flamboyant a congratulatory gesture as I have known her to make. It means a lot.

February 6

Joe Fox telephones. "I just made a bet for you," he says. "The advertising manager, Dan Del Col, predicts that your book will go to No. 1 in the *Times.* For good luck I've bet him a dollar on your behalf that it won't. This way, you stand to win something no matter what happens."

February 7

The editor of one of the big New York City publishing houses writes to Julian Bach asking if I would be interested in writing a book on jumping rope. His professional instinct tells him, he says, that rope-jumping will be the next craze to sweep the country. It is plain that the publishing opportunities are enormous.

I tell Bach I would rather not. For one thing, I know practically nothing about jumping rope, and in any event cannot imagine myself concentrating on the

---

Scandinavian countries. In advances alone I will receive $47,686 from foreign sales—nearly five times the amount of my original Random House advance. Eventually the foreign editions themselves, having been published, arrive in the mail, and in my living room I am able to contemplate a shelf of books that I wrote but cannot read. Surprisingly, two of them, the Australian and Argentinian versions, become No. 1 best sellers in their respective countries.

subject long enough to research and write a book about it.

The request amuses me, however. It wasn't very many months ago that I could hardly find anyone willing enough to publish *The Complete Book of Running.* Now publishers are coming to me.

February 10

It is an icy winter. Manhattan is frosted and rimed, and the sidewalks are rutted with refrozen slush. Because it is impossible to run in Central Park, as I sometimes do when I need to be in the city for a day, I am working out on the rubberized oval track that encircles the balcony of the West Side YMCA's gymnasium. Visible below, on an ancient floor of polished oak, are the members of an exercise class. Dressed in sweatsuits and leotards, they are stretching, flexing and grunting to the cheerfully boisterous commands of their instructor, who has ropelike muscles and a brass whistle.

A man dressed in purple running shorts and a faded yellow T-shirt falls in next to me. He wears an oversized mustache that looks much like the brushes designed for getting at the backs of household radiators.

"Hi there, Jim," he says. "I'm Matty Berrigan. I make television films. I'm good. I was nominated for an Emmy last year, and now I want to create a television show starring you."

As we move along the track, our running shoes slapping its spongy surface, Berrigan describes the show he has in mind. "It will be the greatest thing ever done on running," he says. "Farrah Fawcett will probably be in it if she's free, and Joanne Woodward for sure, and a lot of other big stars. It can't miss. CBS will snap it up in a minute. If not, NBC is sure to take it."

It is imperative, Berrigan goes on, that we move quickly; even as he speaks, the opposition, aware of the growing interest in running, is no doubt planning rival programs.

"It's essential that you and I do this show, rather than someone else," Berrigan says. "We want our film to have true artistic value. Above all, we want to capture the lyricism and poetry of running. That's key."

Berrigan, I notice, is breathing hard. Whether this results from creative excitement or simply from more intense exercise than he is accustomed to, I have no way of determining.

"Also," he goes on, "there is a large amount of money to be made here, an extremely large amount."

Berrigan asks me to join him for lunch. We shower, dress and walk down the street to a restaurant called the Ginger Man. Over a salad Berrigan tells me he will now prepare a so-called treatment, a detailed outline of the program. Then, after a few formalities that need not concern me, we will start work. Shooting should be finished in a few weeks, and it will be only a matter of time before the money arrives in embarrassingly indecent quantities.

Outside the Ginger Man, Berrigan and I shake hands. "I'll be in touch," he says. "Believe me, this is going to be some show."*

February 13

A rumor is reported to me by a worried friend, Van Messner, who with his wife, Nancy, operates a bookstore in Old Greenwich, Connecticut. He has heard, he says, that I have had a heart attack. If this were true, I realize, I would thus, as a ten-mile-a-day run-

*I never hear from Berrigan again.

ner, have presumably invalidated one of the chief health benefits customarily claimed for the sport.

I tell Messner I am feeling fine; I have not suffered so much as a hangnail. I never discover the source of the rumor. A rival running-book writer?

February 14

A television producer named Max Garfinkel telephones. He wants to talk with me about a series on running. We make an appointment for the next day.

February 15

Garfinkel's office is a large one-room penthouse on Third Avenue not far from Fifty-ninth Street. Garfinkel weighs at least 350 pounds, has a physique not unlike King Kong's and is wearing, perhaps in deference to my visit, a purple velour warmup suit and Adidas running shoes. He shows me to a chair of ornate, Spanish Renaissance design, scoops a somnolent Siamese cat out of it and tells me, "The potential is enormous. There is a lot of money to be made here."

A woman's voice comes from across the room. "A lot," it echoes. I am startled; I had supposed us to be alone.

For the first time, I notice the woman. She is in the farthest corner of the room, and she is, unaccountably, in bed, wearing a black nightgown. Garfinkel does not introduce her, nor does he offer to explain what she is doing there. After a while she emerges, puts on a rust-colored fur coat and comes over to talk. She tells me she once worked as an airline stewardess, but now, having discovered under Garfinkel's tutelage that she has an intellectual bent, spends most of her time reading serious literature, chiefly the classics. The last classic she read, she informs me, was *Your Erroneous*

Zones, by Dr. Wayne Dyer. Garfinkel tells her I am a writer. In writing, she volunteers, character is the most important element. I promise I will make an effort to remember this.

Garfinkel says, "I envision a series on running as a global phenomenon. You and I and Rita here will go to Europe, the Far East, Australia, New Zealand—everywhere. The show will be a bombshell. It will make us a fortune."

He says he will draft a proposal and get back to me within a very few days.*

February 16

Book reviewers, I am coming to feel, not infrequently know too much. Despite gloomy appraisals by professional reviewers in two publications, the *New York Times* and *Sports Illustrated,* comments from readers are almost uniformly favorable. Not just letters but telegrams have arrived by the hundreds; their unruly multitude fills several shelves and cardboard cartons in my study.

I find these communications so encouraging and, in their innocent and cheerful hyperbole, so fascinating that I read and answer each one. *The Complete Book of Running* is described as "the best thing to hit the market" and "the most comprehensive book on the topic." A man in St. Petersburg, Florida, writes, "History will let it be known that you and Bill Rodgers and Frank Shorter did more for America than any politician," and the president of an investment banking firm in Manhattan tells me, apparently with a straight face, "Your career has been an inspiration for many." I hear from Senator William Proxmire, from a sixty-

---

*I never hear from Garfinkel again.

seven-year-old jogging nudist in France, and from dozens of ministers, rabbis, schoolchildren, physicians, housewives and incarcerated criminals.

Many tell me they treasure their copies of my book. It is difficult not to find myself agreeing with Benjamin Franklin, who once concluded that "the People were the best judges of my Merit; for they buy my Works."

Not everyone, however, is invariably jubilant when someone they know suddenly becomes noticeably successful. Good fortune, particularly when it exceeds ordinary magnitudes, is like litmus paper; it reveals judgments and jealousies that would otherwise remain comfortably invisible.

Some people are less subject than others to resentments of this sort. A writer friend named Barry Tarshis, who wrote *The Average American Book* and other popular works, asked me the other day how much I expected to earn from *The Complete Book of Running*.

"My agent," I told him, "figures it might go as high as a million and a half."

Tarshis shook his head in wonderment. "Jesus!" he exclaimed. "It's great to see a writer doing so well."

Similarly, Bill Boggs, the host of a New York City television show, told me after the book appeared on the *New York Times* best-seller list, "You're the embodiment of the American dream."

On the other hand, some acquaintances are not so openhearted in their rejoicings. One, a neighbor who is himself an author, congratulates me, then adds, "The only question in my mind is how much better your book might have been if you had taken another five or six months and done a *really* complete job."

February 17

I have been using Roy Fields's bee-pollen tablets for two and a half months now. Apparently curious about my verdict, he telephones. I tell him, truthfully, that I can detect no change in my running ability. Recently, however, a friend, aware I was taking the pollen, assured me that although it is true I run no faster than formerly, I now buzz and flap my arms while I do it.

February 19

The book slips to No. 3. Was Dan Del Col wrong? Has it had its run?

February 22

Joe Fox telephones. "I've got some good news and some bad news," he says. "Which do you want first?"

"The bad news," I tell him.

"The bad news is that you've lost a dollar to Dan Del Col," he says. "The good news is that I've just learned that next Sunday your book will be No. 1 in the *Times.*"

I find the news unbelievable. The book has, it is true, already been listed as the top nonfiction best seller by *Time* magazine. The *New York Times* list, however, is the one that counts. When people refer to the best-seller list, that's the one they mean. Now a book I wrote will be at the very top of it.

March 3

A package arrives in the mail. It is from my mother. It contains a second charm, this one made of gold. On it is engraved: "1st." Accompanying it is a note:

"Sorry for my lack of confidence. Next time I'll be more patient."

We both know, of course, that it is unlikely that there will be a next time. Having a No. 1 best seller is a once-in-a-lifetime occurrence—if you're lucky.

March 6

In moments of triumph, nature mercifully contrives to keep us sane by introducing compensatory humbling forces. I stop in at Barnes & Noble on Fifth Avenue today, thinking it would be interesting to watch customers buy copies of my book. After all, *U.S. News & World Report* has said, "Many bookstores report that James Fixx's *The Complete Book of Running* sells out as fast as it hits the shelves."

In the Barnes & Noble basement, current best sellers are piled by the hundreds in numbered bins, and by this time my book is in the No. 1 bin. It will only be a matter of seconds, I suppose, before I see hordes of eager readers swoop down on it.

I wait, trying to look anonymous; it would hardly do to be observed taking such an unseemly interest in commerce. Finally a man stops in front of the display of books, picks up a copy of *The Complete Book of Running,* opens it and reads a sentence or two. Then, grimacing, he puts it back and walks away.

It is the last time I seek to observe the folkways of my readers.

March 7

A letter arrives from an editor at a New York City publishing house. Her firm, she says, plans to publish a book about running. She wonders, therefore, whether I would be willing to write a brief testimonial about it for use in publicity and advertising. Although

I am surprised that anyone thinks my name might help sell books, I do so.*

March 9

I am in the green room at the *Mike Douglas Show* in Philadelphia. George Harrison and the four members of a popular singing group called the Oak Ridge Boys are also here, waiting for the show to start. Because of trouble with a camera we spend more time than usual in the green room.

George Harrison, square-jawed, richly tanned and expensively dressed, is beyond question the most elegant person in the room. Rather than joining in the general conversation, he stands by himself, looking good. I become curious about why he does not sit down as the rest of us are doing. Finally I get up my nerve, walk over and ask him.

---

*This first book is the beginning of a tide of such requests. Similar letters soon arrive from Holt, Rinehart and Winston, W. W. Norton, Harcourt Brace Jovanovich, Atheneum, Coward McCann & Geoghegan, Houghton Mifflin, Simon & Schuster, St. Martin's Press, McGraw-Hill, Alfred A. Knopf, Crown, Hawthorn Books, Summit Books and Little, Brown, not to mention my own publishers, Random House and Doubleday. In addition to blurbs for several dozen books on running, I am asked to provide laudatory comments for works on heart disease, psychology, physical fitness for children, swimming, diet, obesity, style, dreams, chess, outdoor adventure, cigarette smoking, roller disco and getting ahead in business. For the same purpose I am also provided with an advance copy of a book called *The Man Who Rode His Ten-Speed Bicycle to the Moon.* At first, my resistance being slight under the best of circumstances, I accede to virtually all such requests. In time, however, it occurs to me that a Gresham's Law of endorsements may be setting in, so thereafter I arbitrarily say no to all such inquiries. When Random House was preparing *The Complete Book of Running* for publication, Joseph Heller, the author of *Catch-22* and a well-known jogger, was asked for a blurb. He replied that he had written so many over the years that he would prefer not to do another one. At the time I thought his refusal churlish; after all, it would take only a few minutes to glance at the galleys and write an appropriate sentence or two. Now, however, I understand and, belatedly, not just forgive but applaud Heller.

"Sitting down puts wrinkles in a suit," he explains amiably.

Although I am dressed about as well as I ever am, I suddenly feel disheveled.

March 10–17

Over the past several weeks I have been asked to give a great many speeches. I have been invited to elementary and secondary schools, to hospitals, YMCAs, colleges and universities, and to that most curious and ubiquitous offspring of the running boom, the prerace "clinic." I have also appeared on numerous television programs.

Why I do all this, in view of my continuing apprehension about appearing on television and in public, I do not fully understand. I could, after all, easily say no. Usually I tell myself, and anyone who asks, that it is solely to publicize the book and thus increase sales. Yet I know that it is also because I do not want to surrender, if I can help it, to a weakness that embarrasses me.

So I take Valium in small doses and quietly fight. At a television station in Phoenix, I arrive early for an interview. An aide shows me into the studio and tells me I am free to wait there until the crew is ready. She leaves, and I am alone. I sit down on a couch. The set is dark. The cameras are off. On impulse, I get up, walk over to one of the cameras and, facing the lens, speak to it.

"You can't frighten me," I say aloud, looking into it as if it were someone's eye. Then I stick my tongue out in childish defiance.

The program that day, it turns out, is taped rather than live. Although I have taken a precautionary tranquilizer, I have a suspicion I might have been able to get along without it. Somehow a taped program, in which an audience, no matter how large, will see me later rather than immediately, does not constitute the same threateningly naked exposure as a live appearance.

Although I still have a long way to go, I have finally managed to make at least one useful distinction. I still have not discovered, however, precisely why it is I become anxious whenever I appear on television or make speeches. Many people, after all, regularly do both without difficulty. On a visit to Florida, I ask my mother whether she has any clues to the problem.

She thinks for a while. "When you were young," she says finally, "your father and I were always encouraging you to do more. If, as a baby, you spoke a single word, we tried to get you to say a whole sentence. Because you were our first child, it may be that we were not as relaxed about letting you develop at your own pace as we had become by the time Kitty came along. I suppose you got the feeling that nothing you did was quite good enough."

Her diagnosis makes sense. I can recognize in myself an irrational fear of committing some nameless but quite dreadful mistake. This fear is readily identifiable as irrational because I cannot imagine, diligently as I try, what form a mistake of such forbidding magnitude could possibly take.

March 20

Although Matty Berrigan and Max Garfinkel are, I gather, thoroughly in my past, I continue to learn about the peculiar and sometimes sinister workings of show business. On a commuter train to Manhattan today, I sit with a neighbor who is much involved in television. He tells me that a friend, aware that we are acquainted, has expressed an interest in having me host a sports special.

"I'd be happy to talk with him," I say.

"I can introduce you," he offers. "You understand, of course, that I get thirty percent of whatever you earn from the deal."

Never having encountered such an arrangement— my literary agent, after all, receives only 10 percent— I express surprise.

"In this business," my neighbor tells me, "no one brings two people together for nothing. There's no such thing as a favor."

March 21

"I've never written a letter to a book writer before, but your book is so good I had to say 'thanks.' I never have time to read books. Once I saw yours I made time, and it was worth it."

Written by a U.S. Army sergeant stationed in Italy, those sentences, arriving in the mail today, reflect a recurrent theme: many people, including men, women and our sadly overtelevisioned children, who are not ordinarily at home with books, have nonetheless read mine. Recently a San Francisco physician told me, "You have written one of the best books I have ever read, not just on running but on anything." A woman in Weyauwega, Wisconsin, wrote, "Never have I been able to read a book of any size in one sitting, other than a Harlequin Romance. I not only finished *The Complete Book of Running* in one sitting but missed two meals in the process." Similarly, a sixteen-year-old student at the Shattuck School in Faribault, Minnesota, said, "I would rather read your book than any textbook," while a Long Island corrections officer told me my book is one of his five favorites. (The others, he said, are *The Art of Loving, Siddhartha, The Autobiography of Malcolm X* and *The Prophet.*)

Sydney Smith once wrote, "Praise is the best diet for us, after all." Still, it is occasionally possible for an author to receive too much of a good thing. The other day a letter arrived from a naval enlisted man. He wrote, *"The Complete Book of Running* is one of the most fascinating and well-written books I have ever read."

I could not help myself. I took a pencil and scrawled in the margin: "Poor devil."

March 22

To my surprise I hear today from my first wife, Mary; we have been divorced for several years. Having read that the book is selling so well, she tells me she plans to sue for more money.

I ask how much more she has in mind.

She tells me. It is not a great deal. I am relieved.

A lawsuit, I suggest, will not be necessary. I will send the additional money to her voluntarily.

When you write a best-selling book, I am discovering, you never know quite what curious side effects will come your way.

March 23

The book has been out for five months. Some 430,000 copies have been sold. This means I have earned, even after Julian Bach's commissions, $580,000 in royalties. And that doesn't include book-club earnings or proceeds from the sale of foreign rights.

I now possess, in short, more money than many people earn in a lifetime. Yet for some reason, as I study the figures, I have trouble understanding them or associating them with anything tangible. I don't feel any richer than I did when, working as an editor at

Horizon, it took me a year to earn what I now take in during a single good week.

Only once have I succumbed to the temptation to live beyond what I still feel, despite considerable evidence to the contrary, are my means. One day I drove up to a gasoline pump at Oil City, a self-service gas station, to fill my tank. As I paid the attendant he handed me a flyer offering an introductory $2.50 car wash for only $1.00. I started to crumple it; after all, I've always washed my own car, or else dragooned one of the children into doing the job. Then I thought, What the hell, Fixx, you're a best-selling author. I paid the dollar and, feeling both guilt and a mischievous glee, had Oil City wash the car.

Sometimes I feel uncomfortable having so much money when the people closest to me—my mother and sister, for example—have so much less. One day not long ago, aware of my unease, Kitty told me reassuringly, "This is the life I chose." Although it was a generous and affectionate comment, it did little to diminish my sense of the gulf that has come to lie invisibly between us.

Money discomfits me in other ways as well. At one time I routinely paid the children's educational expenses. Now, however, because I am mindful of the dangers of giving them too much, I have made it clear that I expect them to pay some of their own bills. This year, therefore, John has contributed $2,000 toward college out of summertime busboy earnings, and Steven paid $500 earned at his summer job as a college maintenance worker. Both have pointed out, albeit with ungrudging good cheer, that through good timing their older brother, Paul, got off almost scot-free. In so doing they demonstrated that they have seen through my fatherly inconsistency.

March 24

More reviews arrive. *Running,* one of the leading magazines in the field, calls *The Complete Book of Running* "the best book ever written about the sport." The *Baltimore Sun* says it is "the best of the genre." *Business Week*'s reviewer writes, "Fixx has written what will probably become the jogger's bible, a definitive work."

The review that pleases me most, however, is from the *New England Journal of Medicine.* The writer, a San Diego physician named Harold Elrick, says, "Considering the broad coverage of the subject and the author's nonscientific credentials, there are surprisingly few statements that the knowledgeable physician, physiologist or nutritionist would disagree with. . . . The book is highly recommended to all health professionals."

Although I have been writing for a long time, I have never before experienced such praise. It's great fun, of course, but at the same time I am wary. When I became editor of *McCall's* ten years ago, I noticed how easy it was, by nothing more than a quiet word or two, to induce agreement with my most outrageous opinions, and I also observed how heartily my colleagues were suddenly laughing at even my worst jokes. In time, I discovered, such treatment induces a kind of sensory deprivation; it is almost impossible not to absorb the view that you have inexplicably become as wonderful as people say you are. It is, I saw, a seductive madness, so I am apprehensive now. I can neither relish nor shrug off the praise that comes my way. Instead, I nervously enjoy and spurn it at the same time.

Attention has come from other sources as well. A

neighbor, Mike Galella, called from his car one day, "You're a star!" A woman pedaling by on a bicycle said, "You give the neighborhood a little class." A surgeon friend, Stanley Edelman, told me, "Your book is the standard. It's the *Gray's Anatomy* of running." At Oberlin College a student named Judith Zabarenko wrote her senior honors thesis on, of all things, locutionary devices I unwittingly employed in my book. ("In a narrative, if A refers to an event with an episode E1, that has a non-stative main verb in the preterit or present tense, and then refers to another event with an episode E2, of the same structure, then B will hear A as asserting that the event referred to by E2.") And a horse breeder in Connecticut, Kurt Schneider, told me recently that he has started training his horses according to principles he discovered in *The Complete Book of Running.* The animals, he says, are running faster than ever.

March 25

A reader writes from Winter Park, Florida: "I run with my two German shepherds. They are nine years old, but everyone thinks they're puppies. Running keeps dogs younger, too!"

March 27

Not everyone enjoys *The Complete Book of Running.* Today a letter arrives from a young man who is outspoken in expressing his reservations. He writes, "I can't believe how picky you are! You must lead a terrible life, with all your obnoxious little rules."

His is, happily, only the second unfavorable letter I have received. The first, from a Rochester, New York, dentist named W. Bradford Emery, took me to task for an inadvertently errant sentence: "If you try running and find it worse than a trip to the dentist, perhaps you're one of the people whom nature never intended to run."

Dr. Emery, a runner himself, wrote, "I take serious objection to your analogy between the mental anguish of running and a trip to the dentist. . . . If you find your dental care more traumatic and painful than a good marathon effort, perhaps you should consider seeking more humane and modern dental services."*

March 28

Writing a book that attracts so much attention is like taking geological soundings through the strata of one's past. Since publication I have heard from a man who during high school was my closest friend and from several elementary school classmates (including the one who, forty years after having last seen me, still remembered my eyes). Today letters arrive from two women with whom I was irretrievably in love while in my late teens. Both are widows.

March 29

An assistant dean at a university in Pennsylvania, himself an author, writes that he finds my prose "fluid, understandable and pleasant," and a magazine editor congratulates me on my "effortless style."

Little does he know. Easy writing, a college professor told me years ago, makes hard reading. For me, writing is the most stubbornly recalcitrant of agonies. Although I once turned out an entire chapter of *The Complete Book of Running,* or at least a ragged first

---

*Several months later, in making revisions for the English edition of the book, I remember Dr. Emery's entirely just criticism and amend the phrase to read "an *inept* dentist." There are no complaints from Britain's dentists, not even the inept ones.

draft, in a single long day, a thousand words—three typed sheets—is more typical.

Moreover, the longer I write, the slower the process becomes. When I worked as an editor at *McCall's* and *Life* I was comfortable writing on a humming electric IBM. Once I was writing full-time at home, however, and was less often bedeviled by deadlines, I turned to an ancient 1930s model, at one time my father's, that had a graceful art deco curl molded onto its round bosom; unmotorized, it slowed me down and forced me to take time to examine the words I was using. I found its ungainly gait so congenial that before long I took another retrograde step and turned to writing first drafts in pencil.

Recently Alice, whose ideas have always been more modern than my own, asked me if I might not enjoy owning one of the marvelously versatile computer-operated devices that are now common in newspaper offices; although such machines are expensive, journalist friends who use them say they would not write any other way. I gave the idea some thought but decided against making a change. I cannot promise, in fact, considering the Precambrian direction of my writing practices, that by the time a reader sees these words I will not be contentedly scratching away with a peacock feather. It is effort, not effortlessness, with which I seem to be most comfortable.

April 2

Although for the last couple of weeks H. R. Haldeman's *The Ends of Power* has replaced *The Complete Book of Running* at No. 1 on the *Times* best-seller list, my book reestablishes itself today in the top spot. (Virtue triumphs!) Joe Fox sent me a note yesterday: "Bouncing back! That book is all heart!"

April 3

I receive a letter from a woman named Gail Glanville, an executive at a Providence, Rhode Island, advertising agency. The agency, Creamer Lois FSR, Inc., creates advertising for, among other clients, the Third National Bank in Springfield, Massachusetts. Would I, she asks, be willing to appear in one of the bank's commercials? The assignment would require two days of filming, she says, and would pay "between five thousand and ten thousand dollars."

Since the commercial will be seen only on local stations (and since the fee is so high), I can think of no good reason not to do it.

I telephone Miss Glanville. The commercial, she says, will dramatize the bank's offer of sports equipment to customers who open new accounts. To help publicize the campaign, a five-mile road race will also be held. The bank would like me to be present for that event.

"How much, exactly, are you willing to pay?" I ask her.

"We prefer to pay closer to five thousand dollars than to ten thousand," Miss Glanville says.

"How about a flat seven thousand," I ask, "for the two days of shooting and the race?"

"That sounds fine," she says.

Immediately, seeing how readily she acquiesced, I wish I had asked for more, but the agreement has been made. Anyway, seven thousand dollars seems decent pay for two easy days in front of a camera plus five miles of running; I would, in fact, be perfectly willing to do the running for nothing.

April 4

Talking with Joe Fox, I ask whether *The Complete Book of Running* will still be at the top of the *Times* best-seller list next Sunday. "It must be," he says. "Someone would have mentioned it if it weren't."

The book's sales curve continues to rise. Even Doubleday, which all but rejected it, is now featuring it in the windows of its bookstores. It has occurred to me that *The Complete Book of Running,* having been brought out by a rival publisher, might well be something of an embarrassment to Doubleday. Apparently there is some truth to this. One day recently I was talking with the manager of a bookstore in Greenwich, Connecticut. "A Doubleday salesman was in not long ago," she tells me, "and we got to discussing your book. He said whoever is responsible for losing it for Doubleday should be strung up by the thumbs."

Reader's Digest has also changed its mind about the book. Earlier, it found nothing worth digesting or even nibbling at. Now it has second thoughts and publishes a long excerpt.

April 7

A letter arrives from Sam Vaughan, an old friend who is now Doubleday's publisher. It consists of a single sentence: "We were sure wrong."

I am moved by Vaughan's generous spirit. Although Doubleday had been my publisher for five years before *The Complete Book of Running* appeared, he is the only Doubleday representative I have heard from since the book became a best seller.

April 11

The telephone has become a tyrant. In the book I mentioned the name of the town in Connecticut where

I live, so any reader can easily find my phone number. Hundreds do so. For weeks Alice and I have been unable to finish a meal, or on bad days a bite, without an interruption. Nonetheless, I have resisted applying for an unlisted number; such a measure seems unpleasantly standoffish and undemocratic. Each of us has a breaking point, however. Mine finally came at three o'clock this morning. The telephone next to the bed rang. Sleepily, I felt for the receiver. It was a reader, calling from Austin, Texas.

"Mr. Fixx," he said. "I've just finished reading your book and I couldn't wait to tell you how great it was."

My egalitarianism shattered, I ordered an unlisted number this morning. Hungry as I may be for praise, it would have been perfectly all right with me if the Texas reader had waited another few hours to convey his enthusiasm.

April 14

All the attention my book is receiving is not, I am aware, entirely a spontaneous national outpouring of sentimental affection for a deservedly beloved author. On the contrary, after a while best sellers generate their own excitement, in much the same way some nuclear reactions require a nudge to get them started but thereafter bubble along without additional stimulation. First, a best seller, simply by virtue of its best-sellerdom, is accorded more space in bookstores than other books, and thus elbows aside less vigorous rivals. Second, the author of a best seller, no matter how shamelessly self-appointed an authority he may be, is invariably consulted and quoted as if he really knew what he was talking about.*

---

*Although not all readers are aware of it, self-appointed expertise is endemic among those who write books, including, of course, me. Although it would be uncharitable to document this assertion in detail, the interested

Today a newspaper writer calls to ask my opinion of several pieces of exercise equipment. I tell her I haven't used any of it and therefore can't offer evaluations.

"No problem," she says. "Just tell me what you *think* you'd think if you did try them."

Such expert-chasing, reckless and undeserving though it may be, nonetheless has a salutary effect on a best-selling author's career: it insures that his name and eminence—and, more important, the title of his book—will continue to pop up in the press, reminding readers of its availability.

April 16

A twelve-year-old reader named Beth writes: "I am 5 feet 2 and weigh 126 pounds. Most of my weight is in my rear end. What can I do?"

April 18

I drive up Interstate 91 to Springfield to make the Third National Bank commercial. When the bank, which is on the ground floor of an aging downtown building, closes for business at 3 P.M., a camera crew moves in. In front of the tellers' windows, picnic coolers, backpacks, ten-speed bicycles and copies of *The Complete Book of Running* are arranged—the premiums that will be offered to customers in hopes of inspiring them to open new accounts. Bright lights are turned on. On orders from the director, Dick Hope, I look into the camera lens and begin reciting the lines I have been instructed to memorize. "I'm Jim Fixx," I say. "This is my book, *The Complete Book of Run-*

---

reader may easily do so for himself simply by comparing the academic or professional backgrounds of authors with the subjects they choose to write about.

ning. You can get it free, or at a big saving, right here at Third National Bank. . . ."

Frowning, Hope takes me aside.

"Jim," he says, putting an avuncular arm around my shoulder, "when you're just yourself, being natural, you're fine. When you try to act, you're awful."

Taking Hope's criticism to heart, I soon learn to be natural, or at least to imitate myself being natural. When I worked at *Audience,* we published an article about a rock band that was celebrated for its outrageous stage antics. One of its members was quoted as saying, "We imitate what we're supposed to be." Years later, I understand what he meant.

May 5–6

Alice brings home a copy of a public relations trade journal. It reports that during its first week alone my commercial helped the Third National Bank take in $1,000,000 in new deposits. The next morning a vice president of the bank, Dick Driscoll, telephones to tell me delightedly that the figure has reached $3,000,000.

The success of the commercial astonishes me. I have always been convinced I couldn't sell anything. As a boy I once tried taking orders for *Saturday Evening Post* subscriptions but soon gave up. I was too shy to ask people to part with a nickel a week.

May 14

It is the Sunday of the Third National Bank's road race. Having been so handsomely paid, I cheerfully set out for Springfield again. My car's windshield wipers are flicking away a warm mist; it is a perfect day for running. Turning on the radio, I find a Springfield station. The news comes on. To my surprise I hear that because of the rain the bank has canceled its race. I pull off at the next exit, turn around and drive back home. My daily rate of pay has suddenly taken a sharp turn for the better.

May 21

The book is still No. 1 in the *Times.* I am starting to feel thoroughly at home on my perch there.

May 22

This week the *New Yorker* published a cartoon showing a man sprinting out of a bookstore. He is carrying a copy of my book. Today I encounter a friend, Coyne Maloney, who comments, "Fixx, your magic spell is everywhere. How does it feel to be a cult figure?" I tell him the cult-figure business isn't everything it's cracked up to be—it requires too much night work and overtime.

May 28

Down to No. 2 this week, behind Erma Bombeck's *If Life Is a Bowl of Cherries.* . . . I am not greatly saddened or upset by the decline. The book has, after all, been at the top of the nonfiction list for more than six months.

June 9

Dinah Shore, who is herself a runner, decides to base one of her television shows entirely on running. She invites me to Beverly Hills, where, with a camera crew and a multitude of assistants, we go to a small park encircled by a meandering jogging trail. Miss Shore, who seems a warm and genuinely interested interviewer, opens the show by bursting out of a seven-foot-high paper mockup of *The Complete Book of Running.* Then, after observing that the day's guests are all runners, she interviews Joanne Woodward, Hal Linden of *Barney Miller,* Parker Stevenson of *The Hardy Boys* and me.

I remark to a young assistant on the show that Miss Shore must be a congenial person to work for.

He replies, "She leaves all the details to the staff and pretends not to be aware of what's going on. She knows everything, though, down to the last detail, and whenever it comes to a crunch she gets her way. When she isn't around we call her the Iron Butterfly."

During a break in the shooting I fall into conversation with Joanne Woodward, who with her husband, Paul Newman, owns a house a few miles from my own.

I mention a series of Saturday morning races that take place nearby during the summer and suggest that she might enjoy running in them.

"I've heard about those races," she says wistfully. "I'd like to come to them. If I did, though, somebody would recognize me and soon the photographers would be there, and it wouldn't be any fun for anybody."

There is, I realize, such a thing as too much renown.

July 7

A correspondent and a photographer for an Argentinian women's magazine come to the house to work on a story about me.

"We'd like to take a picture of you and your wife running," the writer says.

I explain that Alice is, unfortunately, at work. Jokingly I suggest that we recruit someone else's wife for the photograph.

"Good idea," the woman says.

A neighbor, Gail Lederer, jogs by, and in the spirit of the jest I invite her to pose with me.

After the picture of Mrs. Lederer and me is taken, the writer says, "We'll just say in the caption that she's your wife. No one in Argentina will know the difference."

"Why don't you just say she's a neighbor?" I suggest.

"We could do that, I guess," the reporter replies. Nonetheless, she sounds dubious.

I have a feeling she went right ahead and did it her own way.

July 12

The *New York Times*'s "Metropolitan Diary" column mentions the book in this fragment, purportedly true, of overheard conversation:

> HUSBAND: A guy was talking about this great book in the elevator today. He got off before I got the title, but everybody dies at the end.
> WIFE: It must have been *The Complete Book of Running.*

July 28–August 15

A telephone call comes from London. It is Christopher MacLehose, an editor at Chatto & Windus, the publishing house that plans to bring out the English version of *The Complete Book of Running.*

"We'd be grateful if you could come over as quickly as possible," he says. "There's quite a bit of work to be done on your manuscript."

The comment puzzles me. After all, the Australian publisher, Outback Press, required no such additional work and in fact simply photographed the text and illustrations in the American version.

"Australians don't mind reading American books," MacLehose explains. "The English, on the other hand, won't hear of it. They demand their own."

I fly to London and spend a week making editorial repairs in a basement apartment at MacLehose's house, which faces a quiet, grassy square not far from the Thames and Houses of Parliament. MacLehose and an engaging young associate, Robert McCrum, whose father is headmaster of Eton and who himself attended Eton and Cambridge, have planned a busy visit for me. I interview several English runners, including Christopher Brasher, who was a teammate of Roger Bannister's in 1954 when Bannister ran the first sub-four-minute mile, am introduced to milk-soaked beef kidneys, and pay a visit to a highly regarded sportsmedicine specialist, John Williams, M.Sc., F.R.C.S., at his Farnham Park Rehabilitation Center in Slough, not far from the walls of Windsor Castle. Williams, a man of vigorous opinions, has prepared himself for our meeting by going through the Random House edition of my book and scrawling in the margins "Bullshit!" and "Balls!" wherever he fails to agree with my research. Despite a good lunch at a nearby pub it is a trying day.*

August 17

Back home, I am running on a street in Old Greenwich, Connecticut. A car comes alongside. I suppose, as often happens, that the occupants want to ask directions. It turns out, however, that they merely hope to

---

*Furthermore, in the end my week in England accomplishes little. Even after I return, this time with Alice, for a week-long publicity tour, the British version of the book sells disappointingly. Part of the problem, apparently, lies with the English attitude toward exercise. Compared with Americans, Britons are exceedingly timid about appearing to be different from their neighbors. I talked with one overweight Englishman who told me, "I ought to do some running, but we live in Wimbledon, you know." I asked him what this had to do with the matter. "Running simply isn't *done* in Wimbledon," he replied.

confirm their hunch. "It's him!" one of them shrieks, whereupon they drive off, satisfied.

August 18–19

A check arrives from Julian Bach. It is for $394,778.34 and represents sales of nearly 300,000 books. (Many more books than this have been sold, but there is an unavoidable lag in the time it takes royalties to filter from bookstore to publisher to agent and finally to me.) I have never seen, or even imagined, so much money—not in my own possession anyway. It looks like something one might come across in the federal budget.

Needing to figure out what to do with it, I telephone an acquaintance whom I will call Arthur Warner. Warner, whom I have known for several years, is an investment advisor whose clients include not only individuals but a number of institutions as well. He attended Princeton and Stanford, and is well spoken and pleasingly cheerful. I am constantly coming across his name and financial opinions in such publications as *Fortune, Business Week* and the *Wall Street Journal.*

"At the present time," Warner says, "I'm not actively soliciting new accounts. On the other hand, since we're old friends, it wouldn't hurt for you to drop by."

Warner and I make an appointment for the next afternoon.

His offices are in an old, thoroughly respectable building. The lobby glistens with marble and polished brass. His reception room, which is presided over by a statuesque blonde woman of throat-catching loveliness, is fitted with a large Impressionist painting of shimmering grays and greens, a good Oriental rug and a mixture of Queen Anne and Chippendale furniture, all of it, so far as I can determine, genuine.

"Were you aware," the receptionist asks me, "that Mr. Warner doesn't read?"

It is not clear to me what she is getting at. Does the poor fellow have dyslexia?

"You mean," I ask, "that he doesn't know *how* to read?"

"Not at all," she says. "He assuredly is capable of reading. He's one of the most brilliant men I've ever had the privilege of knowing. It's just that he doesn't *choose* to read. He finds it confuses him."

Warner, she explains, feels that the essence of investment counseling lies in the practitioner's intuitive ability to foresee long-term trends and thus to profit by them.

"Too much information," she says, "jams his radar. The fewer specific facts his mind is cluttered with, the better his intuition operates. If you think about it, you'll have to admit that it makes a lot of sense."

Warner appears, shows me to his office and hands me a leather loose-leaf notebook containing numerous sheets of graph paper. At the top of each sheet appears the name of an individual, a college or some other variety of institution. Many of the names, I observe, are those of physicians. Each sheet contains points connected by a pair of meandering dotted lines. One line, Warner explains, represents the performance of a stock portfolio for which his firm is responsible. The other, for comparison, reflects the Standard & Poor average. All the lines on the sheets he shows me meander more or less steadily upward from southwest to northeast, but the lines that Warner's intuition has created move at a noticeably more northward angle than the others do.

I show Warner the check from Bach. He inspects it.

"Right now," he says, "I am trying, as I mentioned,

to limit the growth of the company. However, I see your problem and will be pleased to do what I can to help."

He withdraws a gold pen from a holder on his desk and hands it to me. I sign the check over to him.

Warner explains that in addition to the customary brokerage fees, his firm imposes a nominal surcharge of either 1 percent of a portfolio's value or $5,000, whichever is greater. In my case, therefore, the amount will be the minimum $5,000—until, that is, such time as he has caused my account to exceed half a million dollars.

"You won't even notice the surcharge," Warner says, placing a forefinger on one of the ascending dotted lines in the leather notebook. "You're going to be quite surprised at the results your portfolio will soon be showing."

It's a good feeling to have my money so ably attended to.

August 28

An invitation arrives from Doubleday. The company is bringing out *The Harvard Lampoon Big Book of College Life* and is inviting me to a reception at which, according to a press release that is enclosed, I will receive an award:

> The Grand Mal Prix will be presented to James Fixx, author of the best-selling *Complete Book of Running,* for the most embarassing [sic] exploitation of a peer-pressure fad. Mr. Fixx will make remarks and discuss his new books, *The Complete Book of Sitting* and *The Complete Book of Falling,* written to promote a line of carpets and sofa cushions designed by Mrs. Fixx.

I write a note to the Doubleday editor (she shall be nameless here) who invited me to the reception. Its tone, I have to admit, is testy: "When I started work on *The Complete Book of Running* several years ago, an exploitation of a peer-pressure fad simply wasn't possible, since there was no fad, no pressure, and hardly a person out running. I wrote the damn thing simply because I'm a nut on running and thought it would be fun to spend some time fiddling with the subject, obscure though it was."

I do not plan to attend the reception. Nor do I ever hear whether or not they give me my award in absentia.

September 3–21

A representative of Ogilvy & Mather, the advertising agency for American Express credit cards, gets in touch with me. His company, he says, would like to use me in one of its "Do you know me?" commercials; it is prepared to pay a fee of $15,000.

The inquiry startles me. American Express, after all, has used such distinguished men and woman as Senator Sam Ervin, Luciano Pavarotti and Virginia Wade in its commercials. Everyone I talk with agrees it is an impressive series.

I sign a contract. A few days later I fly to Paris on the Concorde and, under the direction of an English television crew, set about making the commercial. The script calls for three locations: the Champs-de-Mars near the Eiffel Tower, a path on the bank of the Seine opposite Notre Dame cathedral, and a sidewalk in front of the American Express office on rue Scribe. The bank of the Seine, I am distressed to see, is paved with cobblestones as large as loaves of bread. I am required to run on these and simultaneously to look in a friendly, relaxed way at the camera while enunciating my lines: "Do you know me? Even though I wrote a best-selling book on running, with most people I need something to jog their memory. . . ." I fear I will stumble and be precipitated into the river.

Afterward an Ogilvy & Mather executive, Bob White, and I take a stroll beneath the chestnut trees in the Tuileries. At an open-air refreshment stand not far from the Louvre we stop for ice cream.

I ask White, "How did American Express happen to pick me for this commercial?"

"We do commercials according to various categories," White explains. "You happened to fit nicely into three categories we were trying to fill. First, you're fairly young. Second, you're an author. Third, you're a sports figure."

Feeling flattered, I am trying to think of an appropriately diffident response when White continues. "Actually," he says, "you're not particularly strong in any one category, but you did help us knock off three of them at one time."

Other business opportunities have also presented themselves recently. A man telephoned the other day to say his company would like to reprint, for a substantial fee, excerpts from *The Complete Book of Running* on rolls of novelty toilet paper. I did not pursue the offer. Somehow the symbolism of the idea troubled me.

I have also been asked to provide endorsements for running shoes and clothing, stopwatches, treadmills, pneumatic shoes, jewelry, foot powder, ice packs, arch supports and electrically operated foot baths. I have declined all these opportunities. So long as I continue to write about running, I want to be able to say what I think without worrying about commercial complications.

The only product I have endorsed, in addition to the American Express card, is Quaker 100% Natural cereal, which I have been eating on and off ever since it was introduced back in 1972.

September 25

Harcourt Brace Jovanovich, apparently hoping to profit from the running-book bandwagon my book seems to be helping to create, recently published a paperback volume under the title *The Complete Jogger*. The jacket design, running legs and all, is so similar to what Random House chose for *The Complete Book of Running* that Joe Fox wrote a letter rebuking Harcourt; imitation, after all, is not just the sincerest form of flattery but can also be the most costly. Clearly unsettled at being caught in the act, Harcourt has promised to come up with a new jacket design.

November 11

A Boston freelance writer, Glenn Rifkin, writes me a long letter. He and Russell Morash, who is responsible for Julia Child's *French Chef* series, hope to produce a six-part series on running. "Your input," Rifkin writes, "would be essential to any product we come up with." I telephone him and express interest.*

November 21

A fourteen-year-old boy writes from Narrows, Virginia. "I am forming a collection of autographs of the most famous persons of our time," he says. "Yours will be an exciting addition to it."

Although I am invariably taken aback by such requests, they arrive regularly now. I never realized autograph collectors were so numerous. Presumably because of heavy competition for desirable signatures,

---

*I never hear from Rifkin again.

some collectors, I discover, have devised inventive techniques for motivating their quarry. Soon after my book appeared, a collector in Illinois wrote to tell me that fire had destroyed his entire collection, amassed with patient effort over the years; he was now attempting to replace as much of it as he could. Moved by his plight, I sent an autograph at once.

Since then, half a dozen or more additional autograph seekers have informed me that their collections, too, have gone up in flames. Autographs, I gather, are peculiarly susceptible to fire. Either that or (cynical and unworthy thought!) the *Autograph Collectors' Newsletter*—for somewhere there must be such a publication—has recommended this method as being particularly effective in stimulating compliance by famous persons of our time.

December 3

In spite of Christopher Lehmann-Haupt's review in the *New York Times,* today the same newspaper generously if schizophrenically lists *The Complete Book of Running* among the "Best Books of 1978," calling it "the leader of the pack of running books." The attention my book continues to receive astonishes me. A publishing trade journal, having compared sales figures, puts it high on the list of "The Top Ten Health Books of the 1970s." One night Johnny Carson mentioned it on his television program, and the next morning Jane Pauley praised it on the *Today* show. During a single week more than a year after publication some 22,000 copies were sold. (In those seven days I thus earned $29,700.) In Sarasota, Florida, the local fire department uses it as a textbook for a physical fitness course, and in Seattle recently a mounted policeman, recognizing me as I ran on the path that hugs the bank of Green Lake, called out, "Hey, you're Jim Fixx,

aren't you? I have your book on my bedside table."
Marc Bloom, who edits a magazine called *The Runner,* telephoned one morning not long ago to arrange
for an interview. He told me, "Frank Shorter invented
running. You invented the running book."

Were I an actor who had deliberately striven for
applause, such attention would be a logically consist-
ent result of my efforts. But I in no way sought it, and
certainly never expected it. I feel like a child who,
digging on the beach for sheer pleasure, discovers
gold.

December 13

A fourth-grade student in Tacoma, Washington,
writes: "As a class project we are collecting autographs of famous people. I chose you because you
know most everything about running. Also, could you
send a pair of Nike running shoes, size 5, please."

As fan letters continue to arrive, a subtheme
emerges: many readers insist that, in one way or another, my book has influenced their lives for the better.
A Vancouver, Washington, man tells me he lost 150
pounds soon after he read it. He writes, "You have
accomplished an incredible amount of good in my life
by adding years of happiness and a sense of purpose."
A twenty-five-year-old Genoa, Illinois, factory worker
says: "My sister and I love you and may owe our lives
—at least a few years—to you." A college student in
Brooklyn, describing himself as "subject to anxiety,
depression and drugs," says, "I believe you have
changed my life."

Of course I am pleased that my book has helped so
many people. I am also surprised; during the months
I spent researching and writing it I was not at all sure
that more than a few running enthusiasts would want
to read it. For some reason, however, the book has

developed a reach that no one foresaw. This is movingly demonstrated in an exchange of correspondence with a young man named George Mize, who lives in Gillespie, Illinois.

In his first letter Mize, a steelworker, writes to tell me that not long ago he weighed 340 pounds. He read my book, started running and now weighs 208; he hopes to persist long enough to reach 180.

I write to Mize, seeking to encourage him in his resolve. Soon afterward he mails me a package—a souvenir that, happily, he no longer has any use for. It is a pair of trousers. The waist measures fifty-four inches.

I have no idea what to do with Mize's pants, yet I am so touched by his gift that I cannot bring myself to discard them.

IV

"This Could Be the Carrot That Will Get Our Foot in the Door"

December 18

I hear from a company that I will call Spectacular
Management. One of Spectacular Management's executives, a man who tells me his name is Monty Casino, telephones from Manhattan to say he has been
pondering my American Express commercial.

"You're a magnificent talent," he says. "I've known
professional actors who didn't have one-tenth the ability you have."

Casino says that although he has not yet had the
privilege of meeting me, he has taken the liberty of
doing some thinking about my career. He regrets, he
says, seeing me misuse my talent, which is clearly so

multifaceted, on the mere writing of books when opportunities that are so much more lucrative and, if he
may say so, so much more prestigious are readily
available. As it happens, he goes on, Spectacular Management is uniquely equipped to help me seize these
opportunities. Would I like to drop by and hear what
he envisions?

December 20

I take the train to the city. Spectacular Management's
offices are in a new building on Third Avenue. Yellow
carpeting, as vivid as a cheese omelet, covers the floor;
the walls and even the ceilings are also carpeted, but
in vivid purple. Here and there, affixed to walnut
plaques on the walls, are displayed phonograph rec-
ords plated with gold. Large, colorful posters depict
the members of rock-and-roll bands. On one such
poster a singer brandishing a sequined guitar has
opened his mouth so wide that his photograph could
be used to illustrate a dental textbook.

Monty Casino comes out to meet me. He is perhaps
forty years old. His hair is dusty gray, not dissimilar
in color to a field mouse's coat, and has been artfully
arranged in long, muscular curls like so many screen-
door springs. His shirt, the shoulders of which bear
epaulets and World War II military insignia, is open
to the breastbone. Three gold chains encircle his
throat. He is barefoot.

"Our clients," he says, gesturing toward the posters. "It is not too much to say that few of them would
be enjoying their present eminence if it were not for
the efforts of Spectacular Management."

Casino shows me to his office. Although it contains
three or four chairs, there is no desk, or for that matter
any of the other furnishings customarily found in business offices. Instead there is a stereophonic record

player that is emitting rock-and-roll music at such thumpingly supercharged volume that I fear it will at any moment shatter into a heap of knobs, switches and meters. A young man and woman, oblivious so far as I can see to our arrival, are seated on the omelet-yellow rug. With his fingertips the man is tapping a small drum in time to the music. The woman is dismembering a meat sandwich with her fingers and washing the fragments down with red wine from a gallon jug.

"Total packaging," Casino says loudly, in order to be heard above the music. I await a verb but none arrives. "Spectacular Management provides a complete, top-to-bottom, front-to-back, inside-and-out service. We relieve you of the necessity to make even the smallest decision."

Sinking into one of the chairs, he says, "I envision Jim Fixx posters, Jim Fixx T-shirts and Jim Fixx novelties of all kinds. You are, of course, familiar with the Mickey Mouse watch?"

As a child, I tell him, I once owned one.

"We envision a Jim Fixx watch as well," he goes on. "The hour and minute hands will be representations of your legs as they appear on the jacket of your book. Take my word for it, this could be a very hot item. You can well anticipate what its reception among joggers would be."

I tell him I certainly can.

Having finished the sandwich, the woman on the rug prepares a joint and begins to smoke. The air in Casino's office grows sweetly aromatic.

"I know you'll agree with me," Casino says, "that this is a most exciting concept. Needless to say, I contemplate, in addition, a wealth of commercial endorsements. Cosmetics. Automobiles. Alcoholic beverages. Cigarettes. We'll have a line of sportswear

bearing your name. There's no question we can move
your career in a whole new direction."

I tell him I can easily see that this might be the case.
I ask whether he will prepare a memorandum outlining the full scope of the program he has in mind so I
can study it at my leisure. A cloud passes over his face.
"We'll have to work fast," he says. "I'm not sure
there'll be time. . . . "*

Odd. I have one advisor, Arthur Warner, who does
not read. Now, if I chose, I could have one who apparently does not write.

December 23

In a playful mood the *Washington Post* publishes a list
entitled "Point System for Hitting Joggers." It reads
as follows:

ONE POINT—Anyone in old-fashioned sweatsuit.

TWO POINTS—Anyone in warmup suit.

FIVE POINTS—Anyone in warmup suit with color-coor-
dinated sweatbands and day-glo jogging shoes.

TEN POINTS—Any couples in matching Bill Rodgers $65
warmup suits, or in matching Frank Shorter $25
shorts.

TWENTY POINTS—Bill Rodgers or Frank Shorter.

FIFTY POINTS—Bill Rodgers *and* Frank Shorter.

ONE HUNDRED POINTS—James Fixx, with or without his
American Express card.

Any publicity, Alice keeps telling me, is good publicity, so long as your name is spelled right.

*I never hear from Casino again. In one way I am sorry to see Monty
Casino and Spectacular Management disappear from my life. It would
have been fun to own a Jim Fixx wristwatch, and interesting to see what
its reception among my fellow joggers would have been. I have a strong
hunch I'm better off not knowing.

December 28

Never before having had anything like the degree of attention I am currently receiving, I do not always respond surefootedly. One writer on the subject has observed: "Famous people work very hard to appear slightly bewildered by all the attention, all the press coverage, all the crowds." Although no one has instructed me in how a celebrity ought to behave, an attitude of bewilderment seems to come more or less naturally, along with an affectation of modesty that to most people apparently seems genuine. A reporter for the *Los Angeles Times* writes of me, "He's as down-to-earth as a celebrity can be," and a Washington, D.C., newspaper headlines a story, "Sudden Wealth Doesn't Affect Fixx." People, both friends and strangers, repeatedly insist that success has not gone to my head, and a customer in a Manhattan bookstore, having asked for and received my autograph, says, "You're just as nice in person as you are in your book."

This, it seems to me, is not entirely true. On the contrary, I have acquired some novel depravities since the appearance of my book. The other day I heard myself grumble to a friend about the quality of chauffeured limousine service. On another occasion, while working at my desk, I looked impatiently at the telephone, which for some time had been silent. *Ring, dammit,* I thought. *Why are they ignoring me this way?* In airports and on streets I surreptitiously study faces to see whether I am recognized, and feel neglected if I am not. Today, when a salesclerk kept me waiting, I thought impatiently: *Doesn't she know who I am?*

Recently it occurred to me that although *People* had interviewed me twice (and had said, among other innocent journalistic exaggerations, "He's got the most celebrated legs since Betty Grable"), its rival, *Us,* had never published a story about me. Slyly I telephoned an old friend named Peter Janssen, who is now editor of *Us,* and invited him to lunch. Although we spent a pleasant hour together, the veiled reminder failed to produce a story. It may be that Janssen saw through my subterfuge and with stubborn good sense decided not to be taken in by it.

December 31

An anniversary—a whole year on the *Times* bestseller list. Having nothing to do for a few minutes, I relax with a collection of poetry. One couplet of Coleridge's "Ode to Tranquillity" reads:

> *Tranquillity! Thou better name*
> *Than all the family of Fame!*

Being well known has undeniable advantages. My bank, for example, not only graciously neglects to charge me the customary $5 penalty when I overdraw my checking account, but goes so far as to cover such checks on its own until I get around to making a deposit. For the most part, however, looking back on this frenetic and not infrequently disorienting period, I find myself heartily agreeing with Coleridge.

Remaining well known is an occupation that could, if I let it, keep me as busy as any conventional job. For despite its considerable candlepower, renown is fragile and, above all, evanescent. One day a woman representing a hospital asks me to give a talk to the doctors and nurses there. I tell her I cannot, explaining that I have another commitment at that hour.

She replies, "Maybe we'll ask you next year—if you're still famous then."

January 7, 1979

Alice and I assemble income tax figures for 1978.
During the year, it turns out, I earned $598,825. Since
we could live in considerable comfort on half a million
dollars less, I hardly know what to make of this
thoroughly unreal figure. It is utterly confusing. If I
see a penny on the pavement while I'm out running I
stop for it. A cleaning woman I know tells me, on the
other hand, that because of inflation she no longer
considers it worth her while to pick up anything less
than a dime. These days few things seem more ambig-
uous than money. I have so much of it, yet in many
ways do not have any idea what it means.

January 12

A sixth-grade student named Robin writes: "Would
you be kind enough to help with our project by sending an autographed picture to place on the wall? The
reason I selected you is because you are a Great Living
Author."

January 30–February 5

The manifestations of being a Great Living Author are
not, I am finding, steady but quite variable. A woman
from New York's *Midday* television program telephones with a request she breathlessly describes as
urgent. She says the show is planning a panel discussion in a few days on what it's like to be a celebrity,
and she wonders whether I am available to participate.

Looking at my calendar, I discover that I have an
appointment at that time with a television producer
who is thinking of making a documentary about running.

The *Midday* representative says she is disappointed.
The program is a particularly important one and my

presence, she and her colleagues feel, is essential to its success.

Flattered, I tell her I will find out whether I can reschedule my appointment with the producer. After making half a dozen telephone calls I finally track him down and shift the appointment. I phone the woman from *Midday* and report that I will be able to appear on the show after all.

She tells me she is extremely pleased, and she knows that the show's host, Bill Boggs, will be happy as well.

The day before the scheduled taping she telephones again, this time to tell me that someone on the *Midday* staff has inadvertently booked one guest too many. One celebrity must therefore be dropped. My presence on the show, she says, is no longer required. My rank in the pecking order is, I am chagrined to observe, quite clear.

This is not the only such incident. In San Francisco not long ago I was scheduled to autograph copies of my book at Macy's. The day before the autographing a woman from the store telephoned me in my room at the St. Francis Hotel. "Are you all ready?" she asked.

I told her I was.

"It's scheduled for ten o'clock," she said. "We'll pick you up at nine forty-five. We're expecting a mob."

The next morning, promptly at 9:45, the telephone in my room rang. It was the woman from Macy's. I told her I would be right down.

In the lobby, to my surprise, I found not just the woman but a store executive named Ron and a uniformed security guard equipped with a two-way radio.

Ron outlined the plan. "To avoid the crowds," he said, "we'll enter the store by the side door. Herb here will open up a path for you if necessary. Should there be any trouble, Herb will call for reinforcements on

the radio. At exactly eleven o'clock we'll leave, again
by the same side door."

Ron looked at his watch. "Okay," he said, "it's
time."

Switching on his radio, Herb spoke into it: "We're
on our way."

We walked down Geary Street and, at 9:59, entered
the store by the appointed entrance. We made our way
to the lower floor. There, a section had been set aside
for the autographing; parallel ropes, affixed to stanch-
ions, indicated where autograph seekers would be required to wait in line. Not a single autograph seeker
was present, however. During the hour I was there
several shoppers finally wandered by; eight or ten
bought copies of my book and asked for autographs,
and one, a jogger, inquired about a knee problem.
When my allotted hour was over the Macy's woman
thanked me for coming. Herb did not accompany me
back to my hotel. "We seem to have overdone the
security precautions," I heard him say as I left.

February 6

A man from the N. W. Ayer advertising agency telephones to ask if I might be available to appear in a
commercial for 7 Up. He does not mention a fee, nor
do I inquire about one. Instead, I telephone a neighbor
whom I will call Fred Simpson; I have heard that he
serves as business manager for a number of athletes.

"These negotiations can be tricky," he says. "You
can lead a horse to water but you can't necessarily get
him to put all his eggs in one basket."

Simpson says that if I like he will get in touch with
N. W. Ayer and see what fee they have in mind. "I'll
sound them out telephonically," he tells me.

If he ultimately conducts negotiations on my behalf,
he goes on, he will be glad, since the offer came di-

rectly to me and was not stimulated by him, to charge
me only 5 percent of whatever I earn instead of his
customary 10 percent.

I ask him to go ahead and take his telephonic
soundings.

February 7

A writer for *Money* magazine, Joe Coyle, comes out
to the house to interview me. Although I have thus far
earned more than half a million dollars in royalties
and, in addition, a good deal more from commercials,
Coyle tells me he is fascinated to see how little my life
has changed since *The Complete Book of Running*
appeared. Under his artful questioning, curiosities,
odd correlations and strange juxtapositions that have
not previously occurred to me emerge.

So far as I can determine, I tell Coyle, the one-dollar
car wash at Oil City has been my only indulgence thus
far. Otherwise, Alice and I live just about as we always
have. One day recently, to save money, I installed a
new toilet in an upstairs bathroom instead of hiring a
plumber to do it for $50 or so. On another occasion
Alice spent most of a summer afternoon selling some
unwanted pieces of furniture at a neighborhood garage sale; she brought home $116. One weekend not
long ago, Robert MacNeil, the co-host of *The Mac-
Neil-Lehrer Report,* and his wife, Jane, came to dinner. Seeing the peeling paint on the walls of one of our
rooms, Jane laughed. "Most people, if they let things
go the way you have," she said, "would be considered
just sloppy. Now that you've got a million dollars,
you're interestingly eccentric."

My reluctance to live up to what have so unexpectedly become my means does not result only from a
failure to understand what those means are. What
prevents my living differently from the way I do is the

vast and growing discrepancy between the amount of money I have and the amount possessed by the people who are most important to me. Recently Kitty told me that because of a succession of unanticipated expenses, her family's savings account was down to $84. (I offered her some money but, characteristically, she declined to accept it.) If, I reasoned, I can manage to live as if I, too, had only $84, instead of ten thousand times that amount, maybe Kitty and I can continue to inhabit the same world—the only world, after all, that I feel at home in.*

February 9

Fred Simpson calls with a report. At first, he says, N. W. Ayer offered $15,000 for my appearance in the 7 Up commercial but was telephonically persuaded to raise the figure to $21,000.

"It's not a great fee for this kind of thing," Simpson says, "but they have plenty of other important clients. This could be the carrot that will get our foot in the door."

I tell him to go ahead with the contract. More than one important advance in civilization, after all, has started with nothing more promising than a carrot in the door.

February 18

By now almost everyone I meet is aware of *The Complete Book of Running.* With John and Alice I fly to New Orleans to run in the Mardi Gras Marathon. At the twenty-mile mark a fellow competitor, badly fatigued, recognizes me and gasps, "I wouldn't be hav-

---

*When he finally writes his article for *Money*, Coyle refers to me as "the tightfisted author of a long-legged bestseller." He is right. What he does not know is that it is chiefly myself with whom I am tightfisted, and that I stay that way out of a tenacious instinct for self-preservation.

ing to go through this agony if it weren't for that silly-ass book of yours." The comment is meant good-naturedly—at least I choose to think so.

All this traveling—promotional appearances, speeches and so forth—is doing very little for my running. In New Orleans, John, who is not yet seventeen years old but has been training hard in preparation for spring track at Greenwich High School, beats me in a marathon for the first time.

It's a paradox. I write a best-selling book on running, yet my own performances become progressively worse. Let's hope not too many readers notice.

March 23

George Plimpton, on assignment for Home Box Office television, arrives at my house in a chauffeur-driven Cadillac limousine. When he steps out of the car I see that he is surprisingly tall, well over six feet. He has a patrician manner that makes me feel, by comparison, like a hayseed, and appears indefinably abstracted, as if his mind were occupied with important concerns. Moreover, he seems not entirely sure what he is supposed to do while he is at my house.

What he is supposed to do, it turns out, is conduct an interview on that perennially popular subject, how to get started in running. While we wait for the camera crew to set up, we talk. He tells me he is still much involved with the *Paris Review,* which he founded a quarter of a century ago. "It's my first love," he says.

I mention how much I enjoyed *Paper Lion,* Plimpton's account of what happened when he, a sports enthusiast but by his own admission an athlete of no great gift, temporarily became an unofficial member of the Detroit Lions football team.

Plimpton seems simultaneously pleased and pained.

"That was almost fifteen years ago," he tells me. "I've written better books since then." Recently he has been thinking of doing another book in the *Paper Lion* mold. It would describe the adventures that occur when a rank nonrunner—Plimpton himself—decides to get into shape and compete in a full-length marathon. What do I think of his writing such a book?

I reply that it seems to me an excellent idea, and one that, so far as I know, has not yet been done. I point out, however, that by the time it can be published two years or so hence, interest in reading about running may have diminished considerably. After all, several hundred books about the sport are already on the market.

Gravely, Plimpton says he sees my point. Not long afterward I read that he has started work on just such a book.

March 26

Being well known, as more than one well-known person has observed, is sometimes as much a nuisance as a pleasure. In the *New York Post* the singer Linda Ronstadt is quoted as lamenting, "As people know who you are and want to gain access to you, you have no choice but to become more isolated. And the more isolated you become the more lonely you become and the more distorted becomes your view of reality." In much the same weary vein, Alex Hailey recently wrote an article for *Playboy* entitled "There Are Days When I Wish It Hadn't Happened."

I can't summon up much sympathy for such celebrities—or for that matter, even on my most difficult days, for myself. At times, it is true, I become more fatigued than I would like to be; sometimes I just want to get away from it all. Even so, I seldom forget that the new pressures in my life are mostly of my own creation, or at least acquiescence. Some people become celebrities by accident; it's not their fault at all. They wake up one day and renown, unbidden, has simply arrived. No one, however, not even the most luminescent of Hollywood stars, is required to play the celebrity game if he would rather not. One does so for no other reason than that one has decided, for whatever reason, that one wants to.

April 3

A woman in New Jersey sends me the lyrics she has written for a song on the subject of running. They consist of three verses, each followed by an identical chorus:

> *Joggin', joggin', joggin', joggin', joggin',*
> *Joggin', joggin', joggin', joggin', joggin'.*

Although I do not tell her so for fear of hurting her feelings, it seems to me that the chorus might benefit from more variety.

April 16

It is the day of the Boston Marathon. The *Good Morning America* people have asked me to come out to the starting line to appear on their show and to interview some of the competitors. Waiting for the program to begin, I notice a middle-aged woman in a beige raincoat standing nearby. She carries a camera and has a pleasant, guileless expression. I have the sense that I have seen her before, and finally I realize who she is: Erma Bombeck, whose deft essays on everyday foibles and crises have made her one of the most widely read authors of our time.

I walk over and introduce myself. "I just wanted to say," I tell her, "how much I've enjoyed your books and columns."

She laughs and thanks me. "Coming from you," she says, "that really means something. Bill, my husband, thinks of you as a saint. He reads your book constantly."

A few days later Mrs. Bombeck mails me a copy of her latest work, *Aunt Erma's Cope Book*. On the flyleaf she inscribes it, "If you don't laugh, I can't bear to hear about it." In Chapter 9, which is entitled "The Complete Book of Jogging," she writes:

> Jim Fixity's legs were the first thing I saw every morning and the last thing I saw every night. They were on the cover of his best seller *The Complete Book of Jogging*. For the past two years my husband had followed the gospel according to St. James Fixit, ate Jim's cereal, took Jim's warming-up exercises, adopted Jim's form, ran with Jim in races whenever he could, and occasionally— when he thought no one was looking—lived out his fantasy by posing his legs in front of the mirror like the legs on the cover of the book.*

May 2

Roy Fields telephones. "How's your supply of bee pollen?" he asks.

"Just fine," I tell him. "I've got plenty left."

He says he will send another 500 tablets.

May 24

A woman writes from Miami, Florida: "Recently my entire autograph collection was destroyed in a tragic fire. . . . "

---

*Several months afterward, at the Burbank Studios in Los Angeles, I encounter Mrs. Bombeck when she appears on the Johnny Carson show. She says, "I was scared to death you might decide to sue me after you'd read Chapter 9." "Of course not," I tell her. "But if you'd been around at the time I might have hugged you."

June 5

It is a busy day for interviews—three in the morning, two in the afternoon. In the year and a half since the book was published I have been interviewed more than a hundred times. The pleasure I derive from such sessions varies, depending on the inventiveness and intelligence of the interviewers, as well as the amount of advance research they have done. Many ask, "How did you get started running?" when the answer, in all the detail I can possibly provide, is spelled out in the first few pages of *The Complete Book of Running.* If an interview begins this way, I know I'm in for a bad time. Frequently the journalist has not read, or even opened, the book. At a television studio in San Francisco I was scheduled to tape a segment to be used on a news show. The program was co-hosted by a man and a woman.

"Do you live here in San Francisco?" the woman asked as we waited to begin.

"No," I told her, "in Connecticut."

"What exactly brings you out here?" her colleague asked.

After several such inquiries, the co-hosts looked at each other helplessly and started laughing. "Mr. Fixx," one of them finally confessed, "we don't have the slightest idea who you are or what you're doing here."

Styles of interviewing vary greatly. Larry Batson of the *Minneapolis Tribune* told me he finds that if he simply acts confused and helpless, most of his subjects take pity on him and come to his rescue with usable facts and quotations. Other reporters leave less to chance than does Batson, that trusting soul. The most dictatorial interviewer I have encountered is a *News-*

week writer, Susan Cheever Cowley. Rather than ask questions in the conventional manner, she simply ordered me: "Now do how you began running. . . . Now do when you were starting out in journalism. . . . Now do how you wrote the book." I had an uneasy feeling that a failure to comply might have unpleasant consequences.

Among the most skillful of the interviewers I have met is a *New York Times* reporter, Anna Quindlen, who spent a morning at my house recently. Soft-spoken and earnest, she seemed not so much interrogator as guest. Furthermore, without badgering or boring in, she gathered material for one of the most comprehensive and accurate stories I have thus far seen.

Many reporters seem less interested in what I actually did—sat at my desk long enough to write a book—than in what they want me to be or hope I am. Recently a newspaper clipping arrived from San Diego in which the reporter asserted that I was "thriving on life in the fast lane," when in fact, at the time I spoke with him, I was doing nothing of the sort but was impatient and ill-tempered as a consequence of too much travel and was restlessly hoping to find a lane significantly slower than the one in which I was so reluctantly moving.

I am not, of course, the first person to have noticed a discrepancy between what he is and what people suppose he is. On a flight to San Francisco recently I found myself seated next to Louise Erickson, who as a teenager in the 1940s starred in the popular radio series *A Date with Judy.* She told me, "The fans didn't have any idea who I was. I acted the way they wanted me to act. It was all role-playing."

There is a danger here, and one observer has expressed it this way: "Any person who has reached

tremendous heights of success functions with a different personality with the public, and after a while he
learns to carry that personality with him and finds that
he cannot feel comfortable out of that role, so he
avoids the people who know him from the past."

So far as I am aware, this hasn't happened to me—
not yet anyway. On the contrary, as centrifugal forces
attempt to hurl me away from familiar places and
people, I find myself trying harder than ever to hold
on to old friends and thus to secure myself more safely
to what I know best. Twenty years ago, as a junior
editor at *Saturday Review,* I shared an office with an
editor named Hal Bowser. He was one of the wisest
and most widely read people I had ever met, and we
have been friends ever since. After *The Complete Book
of Running* was published we saw each other less
frequently than we once had. Invariably, however,
after a few weeks without seeing him, I find myself
craving his company and get in touch with him. An
hour or two of conversation never fails to restore my
sense of who I am and, just as important, who I want
to avoid becoming if I can.

July 3

A letter arrives from a doctor in Missouri. He writes,
"Continue your good work, Mr. Fixx. You as a lay
person have accomplished more in preventive medicine than I ever hope to accomplish in my field."

So many people have made similar observations
that I am almost coming to believe them.

July 26

Erma Bombeck is at it again, this time in her syn-
dicated column. She declares my legs "Most Sensuous
in the Literary Field."

"Legs," she writes, "have not had such an impact

on the American way of life since the two hind ones of Mrs. O'Leary's cow kicked over the lantern in Chicago in 1871."

August 9

I have been invited to Washington, D.C., to participate in a panel discussion on health and exercise at the Kennedy Center. My fellow panelists, I have been told, will be Dr. Robert Linn, author of *The Last Chance Diet,* and Dr. Herman Tarnower, creator of the Scarsdale Diet.

I fly to Washington. Backstage at the Kennedy Center, the moderator, Judy Bachrach, who is a writer for the *Washington Star,* explains the session's format. As she talks, Tarnower, who is tall and has a courtly manner, interrupts.

"Miss Bachrach," he says ingratiatingly, "I have always been under the impression that newspapers chose their reporters for their writing ability and not, as is clearly the case with you, for their good looks."

Visibly taken aback by Tarnower's flirtatious comment, Miss Bachrach, looking uncomfortable, goes ahead with her explanation.*

August 10

A *Washington Star* reporter, Jurate Kazickas, interviews me.

"What happens when you go out on the road?" she asks. "Do women proposition you?"

Sometimes, I answer—or at any rate I *think* they do.

In Los Angeles, for example, an attractive woman –

*Eight months later Tarnower will be dead, having been shot in the bedroom of his home in Purchase, New York, by Jean Harris, who is headmaster of a girls' school across the Potomac, not far from the building in which our panel discussion was held.

said, "You have the most beautiful smile. You should make it work for you."

On an airplane bound for Salt Lake City the woman in the seat next to mine, who had told me she was twenty-four years old and worked as a clinical psychologist, startled me by murmuring, "My present sexual preference is heterosexual."

At least by implication, or perhaps only in my steamy middle-aged imagination, there were other such opportunities as well. I was asked to address a singles conference in Newport Beach, California, and to visit a coed health spa up the coast in Mill Valley. The man who invited me to the spa said pointedly, "All the woman who belong to the spa are tens."

However, running does not invariably enhance one's sex life. A sixty-two-year-old man living in Panama wrote the other day to lament that, contrary to my assertion in *The Complete Book of Running,* his five months at the sport had done nothing for his sexual capacities. "My sexual activity has diminished instead of increasing," he reported. "With a tired body there is not much incentive toward participating in sex. However, now that the habit of running is well ingrained, I plan to run only every *other* day, hoping that thusly I will be less tired and hopefully more provoked toward intercourse."

August 25

I run in a 10,000-meter race in Westport, Connecticut. Afterward a young woman asks me to autograph her copy of *The Complete Book of Running.* As I write my name she asks, "What's it like being one of the immortals?"

As I reflect on her semifacetious question, I realize that it is the book, rather than the person who wrote it, that is the chief celebrity. Even my television commercials, in which my face is so nakedly and publicly displayed, have a strange remoteness, as if a second Jim Fixx, unrelated to me, had somehow been cloned.

I try to tell the woman something of the oddness I feel. She replies, "When Joe Namath wakes up in the morning he knows he has to be Joe Namath all day long. I hope you don't have to be Jim Fixx."

Most of the time, I tell her, I don't feel that I do. Nor, I suspect, does the private Joe Namath always have to be compatible with the public Joe Namath. In all likelihood such an invariable identification exists mostly in the minds of celebrity watchers who do not themselves know any celebrities very well. When I am alone, so far as I can see, I am pretty much the person I have always been; being well known is the last thing on my mind. I can think of no reason why the same would not be true of Namath, Elizabeth Taylor or Senator Kennedy.

September 16

No. 12 in the *Times*. Twenty-two months on the best-seller list—though at this point the book can hardly be said to be very secure. It is, in fact, barely clinging by its toenails.

September 20

A few days ago President Carter, running in a 10,000-meter race near Camp David, collapsed and had to be helped by the Secret Service men who accompanied him. Describing the mishap, *Time* reported that Carter was particularly puzzled by his disappointing performance since he had trained according to principles set forth in *The Complete Book of Running.* I've been holding my breath, fearing that the unfavorable White House publicity might cause sales to dry up. Joe Fox tells me, however, that the book, while admittedly selling less vigorously than at its peak several months ago, has shown no unusual sag.

October 4

From Europe, Julian Bach sends a cable: OFFICE IN-FORMS OFF TIMES BUT PERMANENT CONGRATULA-TIONS BEING SUCH A GREAT CHAMPION STOP YOU'RE STILL NUMBER ONE ON MY LIST.

Sunday, October 7, will be the first time in nearly two years that *The Complete Book of Running* has not appeared on the *Times* best-seller list. I feel like the Cheshire cat, faded now to nothing but grin.

October 5

During the past several months I have been asked to provide forewords to a dozen or more books, including one called *Marathon Mom* that was written by a mother of quadruplets, and another that was published by a firm in London. If, in fact, I were simply to set out to perform all the tasks that people ask of me I would be in a fever of activity seven long days a week. Within a single week I have been asked, among other requests, to contribute recipes to a cookbook, to serve as honorary starter of a race sponsored by a weight-loss clinic in New Jersey, to sit on several boards of directors, to be honorary chairman of the Connecticut Lung Association, to provide career counseling for countless out-of-work runners, to lecture at a solemn conclave of the Automotive Whole-salers Association of New England, to inspect and presumably buy a $700 watercolor of a running shoe, to offer critiques of numerous unpublished sports books, and to moderate a panel discussion featuring Cheryl Tiegs, George McGovern and other celebrities.

Several times I have also been asked to provide personal mementos for auction at charity benefits. In response to one such request, from the Cohasset, Massachusetts, Historical Society, I mailed off a wrinkled cardboard number worn in an unimportant ten-kilometer race. In the mail today I receive a thank-you letter. The number brought $13.

October 6

A report arrives from Arthur Warner. Mysteriously, the dotted lines on his graphs are losing much of their energy; they have begun to meander in more nearly horizontal paths and even, here and there, to sag earthward like frowns. In an explanatory letter Warner points out that there are unavoidable reasons for the trends: " . . . problems in Iran . . . rising oil prices . . . higher inflation . . . the feverish rise in the price of gold . . . The world has been standing on its head lately."

I am apprehensive. The royalties I have received, abundant though they are, have been a freakish windfall and are almost certainly unrepeatable. I am more eager, therefore, to hold on to what I have than to take risks in hope of dramatic multiplications.

Looking at the graphs, I am not sure that Warner fully understands this. I write him a letter, telling him, "It is very likely that after all the hoopla from my book quiets down, I will go right back to being the obscure fellow I have always so deservedly been—and that my income will decline correspondingly. Our first goal, therefore, must be to preserve."

October 11

Warner replies, saying he understands what I am hoping for and will adjust the portfolio accordingly. Meanwhile, he also writes, he has decided to broaden his understanding of international finance, and thereby enhance his value to his clients, by spending much of the ensuing year in Rome. "It is intriguing," he says, "to be able to compare the value parameters of a stock like Kellogg with one in the Italian pasta industry."

I find myself earnestly hoping that Warner's stay in Rome will restore some of our portfolio's vitality.

October 12–13

I am in Washington, D.C., to make a speech to the National Jogging Association, and then, the next morning, to run in a race sponsored by the same organization. After the speech Bill Palmer of the NJA tells me, "Richard Lugar, the junior senator from Indiana, is extremely enthusiastic about physical fitness. He's anxious to meet you and wondered if you might be able to have breakfast with him at six-thirty tomorrow morning."

Stretching the truth, I tell him that 6:30 is an ideal hour.

Later, however, Palmer phones to report apologetically that because of a conflict in his schedule the senator will not, unfortunately, be able to join me for breakfast.

After I have gone to sleep, a second call comes. It is Palmer again. The meeting, I will be pleased to learn, is going to take place after all. Senator Lugar will pick me up in his limousine in front of the hotel at 6:30.

The next morning I wait for nearly an hour. Senator Lugar never appears, nor do I ever hear either from him or from Palmer about our breakfast.

An hour before my speech in Washington I take a Valium as usual. Yet, standing there in front of an audience of several hundred people, I am aware for the first time of feeling different. Although I have never before articulated the fact, in previous speeches I have imagined audiences as inherently unfriendly, at least at the start, and have seen it as my task to deflect their hostility if I could, to win them over with jokes, anecdotes, a pleasing manner. Today, for no apparent reason, I feel that the audience is entirely sympathetic and I now realize that earlier audiences have also been this way. I look at the faces before me. As I talk, I can see that they are glad to be here listening to me. I think: *They like me!* The moment this thought comes to me, I know it is a milestone in my liberation from the terrors that began so many months ago at the *A.M. Chicago* studios.

October 15

An eleven-year-old Portland, Oregon, boy named Rick writes, "I would like to read your book but I don't got the money. Have a nice day."

V

"People Need to Believe in You"

October 19

At a scientific conference in Manhattan I meet a psychiatrist from Miami, Paul Jarrett, and we have lunch together at a Chinese restaurant. While we eat I describe my contradictory reactions to the money I have earned and my reporter's curiosity about them. I ask Jarrett whether he thinks a psychiatrist might be able to resolve this curiosity by helping me sort out my feelings with more precision than I am able to muster on my own.

Jarrett replies, "Talking with a psychiatrist might tell you something you didn't already know, but you'd have to be sure to go to someone who has dealt with

people in situations like yours. Otherwise he might be
jealous of you or in awe of what you've accomplished.
How about Woody Allen's psychiatrist?"

October 25

I watch *Good Morning America*. Talking about his
father, Kirk Douglas's son says that despite his fame
he still fixes his own morning coffee and continues in
other ways to demonstrate that he "has no way of
identifying just how popular he is."

More clearly than many viewers, I suspect, I understand what the actor's son is talking about. Although
I know that my book, and hence its author, too, have
in some way become "popular," I have no means of
assigning a magnitude to this popularity. Nor, in fact,
am I ever able to perceive it directly. Instead, I see
only reflections. I have come to feel, in fact, that renown may ultimately be little more than reflections,
since a person who possesses it does not—and in the
nature of things perhaps cannot—view its substance.
He views only its effects and concomitants: applause,
adulation, novel annoyances. Fame, strangely, is most
readily detectable by those safely removed from it.

A woman I know unwittingly illuminates this paradox by asking me, "How do you enjoy being famous?"

Thinking about her question, I realize that my telephone rings much more often than it once did, that I
receive much more mail and that I spend much more
time on airplanes. Otherwise, so far as I can see, being
well known isn't noticeably different from being perfectly unknown.

October 31

David Hartman, the host of *Good Morning America,*
telephones. He says he has just been talking with
Phoebe Snow, the singer.

"She'd love to talk with you," he says. "You're her hero."

I telephone Miss Snow, who says, "You're about No. 6 on the list of the most important people in my life. You have no idea what you've done for me. I can't believe I'm talking with you."

November 28–December 4

A television producer, Jeff Wheat, telephones from Hollywood. He is planning a weekly half-hour series to be called *Run for It* and wonders if I would be willing to serve as the show's host. He mails me an outline:

> . . . The first group of runners is seen jogging along a river bank in Detroit, Michigan. As they run, they each announce who they are, where they are from, and then in unison say, " . . . and we're running for it" and hold up their thumbs.

I tell Wheat his idea seems to me to need refining. He says he agrees and will be in touch again as soon as he has accomplished the necessary work.*

January 5, 1980

Just as we did last year, Alice and I gather figures for our income tax return, and I discover that I earned more than $900,000 during 1979. If I did nothing more imaginative than keep it in a bank at 6 percent interest, I would enjoy an annual income of $54,000 —just over twice what I earned as managing editor of *Horizon.*

January 12

In *Making It,* Norman Podhoretz writes, "On the one hand, our culture teaches us to shape our lives in

---

*I never hear from Wheat again.

accordance with the hunger for worldly things; on the other hand, it spitefully contrives to make us ashamed of the presence of those hungers in ourselves and to deprive us as far as possible of any pleasure in their satisfaction." When money first began to come into my life in almost uncountable quantities I felt only pleasure. For the first time I could pay college tuition bills without complex financial siphonings beforehand; I was able to enroll Stephen in a private school; I could buy my mother a new car to replace her sixteen-year-old model. I even enjoyed, although I hoped no one noticed, public allusions to the money I was making. (One magazine, for example, referred to me as "running all the way to the bank.")

An incidental enjoyment lay in finally coming to understand, with the help of an insight from Alice, why journalists were so profoundly fascinated by *my* money. I had noticed, after all, that it is possible to read about many celebrities—Tiny Tim, say, or Evel Knievel—without encountering speculations about their income. For some reason, however, practically every interviewer I have met has asked me, often before he has even taken his coat off, about the money I have earned. When one reporter for a national magazine talked with me, his first question was: "When did you realize that the book had made you a millionaire?" Alice finally suggested that the fascination he and other journalists display may come from the simple fact that we are all doing pretty much the same thing: sitting at a typewriter. Because few journalists sing falsetto or break their bones for a living, as Tiny Tim and Evel Knievel do, comparative judgments are not automatically called into play in writing about them. But every journalist not only knows what I do but can more or less do it, too.

The innocent pleasure I experienced when I first

began to accumulate money did not last long. For one thing, money brings an inescapable psychological distance. Tonight I witness a clear example. Old friends, Bob and Betsy Pearson, are driving Alice and me home from a party in Manhattan. As we travel north, through suburbs populated mostly by corporation executives and their families, our conversation turns to the nature of work in the United States. I suggest, more playfully than in seriousness, that the quality of most people's work would improve if they did less of it. When I worked in editorial offices, I tell the Pearsons, custom decreed that I write or edit for seven or eight hours a day. Now, I continue, I feel I work more effectively even though on many days I am at my desk only half that long.

Pearson, who is a former oil company executive, snorts, "You don't *have* to be at your desk any longer than that. You're a millionaire!"

Although everyone in the car laughs, I am uneasily aware that Pearson's observation, so quick in coming, reflects a difference between us that is as apparent as the different colors of our eyes.

Another friend, one with whom I once spoke on the telephone two or three times a week, has now become too busy for our conversations. I mentioned this not long ago to a woman whose intuitions I have always found trustworthy. Her opinion: jealousy. I am not so sure. Because of its tantalizing glitter, I think, money makes those who have it seem somehow different, as if they had unaccountably turned radioactive.

It also creates an unfair paradox. When a person has little of it, it is likely to be difficult to earn more. When he has a lot, it becomes astonishingly easy. Recently I was asked to make a speech at the annual dinner of a YMCA in New Jersey. Since no fee was mentioned, I welcomed the occasion as a chance to do a good turn. At the end of the evening, to my surprise, I was handed an envelope containing a check for $1,000. (I mailed it back the next morning.) Not long afterward I spent half an hour in a recording studio, dubbing a few lines for a commercial I had made earlier, and received $2,500—more per working minute than my first job after college brought me in a week. And when American Express, having used me in its "Do you know me?" commercial, wanted to photograph me for a follow-up magazine layout, the company's advertising agency offered $1,000. I explained that I was working on a book (I was) and was too busy. The agency raised its offer to $7,500. I cheerfully laid my writing aside for a morning.

Furthermore, although I once experienced no little difficulty in finding a market for what I wrote, I now have in my files book contracts that will bring me, over the next two or three years, several hundred thousand dollars in advances alone.*

The amounts of money I am earning are, in short, large by any standards but a Rockefeller's. Not long ago, when I went to Los Angeles to make the 7 Up commercial, Jim Rice of the Red Sox, Tony Dorsett of the Dallas Cowboys and the superstar jockey Darrel McHargue were my fellow performers. An exuberantly outspoken photographer assigned to take our picture said, "I make good money compared to most people, but you guys sure outclass me. How much did you all make last year?"

We told him. I was surprised to discover that I, a middle-aged writer who is in no way a sports hero, earned more than any of the others.

*They are for a) a companion volume to *The Complete Book of Running* called *Jim Fixx's Second Book of Running,* b) an annual runner's diary called *The Complete Runner's Day-by-Day Log and Calendar* and c) the present book.

January 29

I take my car to a garage for a tuneup. Recognizing me, a customer says, "You saved my life." A year ago, he tells me, he weighed 240 pounds. Now he runs five miles every morning and weighs 150.

Although comments like his touch me greatly, they also strike me as curious. When I wrote *The Complete Book of Running* I had no thought of trying to improve the health of large numbers of men and women. Yet, I am told by many people (including quite a few doctors), this is what I have done.

Is it odd that I cannot bring myself to feel much connection with this accomplishment? It seems to me too accidental for pride or self-satisfaction. In fact, whenever I think of the book's effects, they seem mysterious, a gift. If, on account of them, a few sons today are not required to undergo the same experience I did when my father died at the age of forty-three, I will feel more thoroughly rewarded than any writer deserves to be. Yet I cannot forget that the reward, like the accomplishment, is almost entirely accidental.

February 15

Other preoccupations have prevented my looking up Woody Allen's psychiatrist, or anyone else's, for that matter. Today, however, at a resort on the Atlantic near Charleston, South Carolina, I meet a perceptive psychologist, Dr. Lois Veronen. I ask her, as I had Paul Jarrett, whether she thinks it might help satisfy my curiosity if I were to talk with a psychiatrist.

"No," she says emphatically. "No psychiatrist would believe that you were just curious. The assumption would be that you were troubled in some way, even if you didn't say so. Psychiatrists are taught to think pathology."

Instead, Dr. Veronen suggests, I can easily conduct
a rudimentary self-assessment by considering such
questions as these:

1. In what ways has the satisfaction I derive from
   my customary activities changed?
2. How has my self-esteem changed?
3. How have my expectations for myself changed?
4. In what ways has my pleasure in personal in-
   teractions changed?

I think her questions over.

First, my satisfaction with much that I do is
unquestionably greater than it once was, if only because I am now required to do so few things that I
don't care to do. In particular, the pleasure I find in
my work has been greatly enhanced because I no
longer have to write under forced draft, as magazine
journalists so often must, but each day can produce
whatever amount comes comfortably. When I am too
tired to continue working, I simply stop instead of
having to flog myself to do more.

As for my self-esteem, so far as I can tell it has
changed little since the appearance of my book. For
one thing, since I am aware of the considerable role
luck and good timing have played, I can't take much
credit for its success. But I certainly have no less
self-esteem than I once had.

My expectations, by contrast, have changed noticeably. I demand more of myself and am more readily
dissatisfied if the quality of what I do is less than I
think it ought to be. In other aspects of my life I feel
a considerable unfolding of possibilities. I am able to
choose my friends from a wider range than I once
could, and I can foresee a time when I will be able to
live pretty much where and how I want to.

It is in personal relationships, Dr. Veronen's fourth

category, that my life has changed most noticeably. Not long ago a neighbor, a businessman I had met only once or twice, telephoned to ask whether I was planning to go running. If so, he said, he would enjoy coming along. We headed down a country road that meanders along a river bank. Five miles from home he asked whether I would be willing to invest $25,000 in a nightclub in which he was involved. A few minutes later we turned and started back, but I had to listen to his importunings for another five miles.

Except with my family, a few old friends, and people so richly aglow with celebrity that they plainly have nothing to gain from knowing me, I find it difficult now to avoid a watchfulness that is not exactly compatible with sound relationships.

I wonder whether someone else would have handled all this more gracefully than I have. Like immunity to poison ivy, I suspect, tolerance to financial good fortune is by no means apportioned equally. The other day I came across a book by a professor at the State University of New York, H. Leroy Kaplan. In conducting research for his book, Kaplan talked with more than 100 people who had won up to a million dollars in lotteries. He discovered that while many of the winners found the experience profoundly upsetting ("All I want to do is forget," one said), others remained cheerful and apparently unscathed. Furthermore, there seemed to be no way to foretell which winners, once they had their money, would fall into which category. So it is, too, I suspect, with money that comes from other sources. We simply do not know—not until it happens, anyway—how we will behave. Suddenly possessing a lot of money is not unlike riding a unicycle. Nobody does it right the first time, but some people catch on considerably faster than others. (Some people, of course, never catch on at all.)

March 5

In San Francisco again, I telephone a friend named Ralph Paffenbarger, who is a professor at Stanford and a distinguished epidemiologist; his findings about the causes of heart attack and various other diseases have been among the significant medical discoveries of the past decade. He is having some friends in for dinner tonight and invites me to join them and to spend the night at his house in Berkeley. He tells me, "Having you at the party will do a lot for my reputation."

March 6

Waiting for an airport limousine in Berkeley, I notice a young man studying me. Finally he walks over and asks, "Did anyone ever tell you that you look like Jim Fixx?"

"Yes," I say. "Several people have mentioned that to me."

"It's true," he tells me. "You do."

It does not occur to him that I might be exactly who I appear to be. By definition, celebrities are always somewhere else.

I am unfailingly fascinated by the way historical figures have viewed celebrity. In his essay "The Love of Fame," Samuel Johnson suggests that the concept of fame has undergone important alterations during the past two centuries. When Johnson wrote, fame was chiefly a posthumous benefit—"being celebrated by generations to come by praises which we shall not hear." Thus, although fame in the eighteenth century might have required no small effort in the getting, it asked no attention thereafter. Today, of course, the opposite is true.

I see, therefore, that I have a choice. I can either turn back to my work and watch my well-knownness, unattended, disappear, or I can feed my well-knownness and let my work suffer. The choice seems to me a significant one, for renown has not invariably been kind to writers. Norman Mailer and Truman Capote have deftly solved the dilemma by attracting attention in shamelessly nonliterary ways in between thoroughly serious books. I am neither so versatile nor so tireless as they are. Soon after *The Complete Book of Running* came out I was invited to a party at Barbara Rockefeller's apartment overlooking Central Park. The affair was replete with champagne, important people and celebrity gossip in quantities large enough to satisfy the most insatiable eavesdropper. Photographers from the newspapers and magazines were there, and the next day my name was mentioned as one of those who had been present. Having stayed up too late, however, and enjoyed myself too unreservedly, I sat at home with crimson eyes and a headache, unable to do a decent day's work.

Such disabilities, I am coming to believe, are among the inevitable by-products of trying to stay well known. Writers need nothing so much as a good early curfew.

March 10–24

I am running through Centennial Park in Sydney, Australia, a vast and lovely acreage of lawns, woods and bridle paths. Near a pond noisily aflutter with Australasian waterfowl, my path and that of another runner, a man bouncing energetically along, merge. We begin to talk as we run and, hearing my American accent, he says (pronouncing my first name to rhyme with *limes*), "You must be James Fixx. You have quite a cult here."

The man, a lawyer, is not surprised to find me in Sydney because my photograph, four columns wide and dominating the top of page 1, has just appeared in the *Morning Herald.* It is there, along with an article, because *The Complete Book of Running* is in its eighth printing here and has sold nearly 45,000 copies, an almost unprecedented number, I am told, by Australian bookselling standards. Indeed, as I discover when I arrive after a twenty-hour journey, it is as well known here as it is at home; like their New Zealand neighbors, Australians are prodigiously enthusiastic sportsmen. I am asked to appear on television, am interviewed on radio programs, and address several organizations. On streets in Melbourne, Brisbane and Sydney passers-by say hello to me, and in the lobby of one hotel a placard reads "Welcome, Jim Fixx."

Still another curiosity about the visit to Australia is that it costs me nothing. Every last penny of it— first-class air fare, meals and, when a day's work is finally done, a few cans of excellent Australian beer— is provided by my Australian publisher, Outback Press. If the rich do not invariably get richer, neither do they necessarily get poorer, as other people must whenever they decide to travel halfway around the world.*

On my last night in Sydney I am invited to a party at the home of Mike Agostini, who earned a gold medal as a sprinter in the 1954 Commonwealth Games. He

---

*Months later, the trip offers another financial curiosity. Outback Press, having fallen on hard times, is unable to pay the royalties it owes me. The amount not paid, my agent reports, is more than $22,000.

was nineteen years old at the time, and is forty-four now. Agostini, who has a quick, cheerful manner, lives with his wife, Pamela, and four children in a suburb called Vaucluse, which clings to a slope overlooking Sydney Harbor. From his balcony much of the city, including the Harbour Bridge and the celebrated puffin's-beak Opera House, can be seen glistening in moonlight. Agostini, who now works as a publisher of sports magazines, and I sit on his balcony drinking pungent Tasmanian beer. It is March—late summer in the Southern Hemisphere—and as warm in the night wind as the inside of a wallaroo's pouch.

"When I was nineteen," Agostini says, "I was as well known in the Commonwealth as you are in the United States. I was quite famous. I know what fame can do to a person. Don't ever let yourself think that all the recognition you're getting is really you. People need to believe in you, so let them. But it's fatal if you start believing all the wonderful things you hear about yourself."

Long after I leave Sydney I find myself meditating on Agostini's words.

March 27

Going through the accumulated mail, I look at a report that Alice and I have received from Arthur Warner. The dotted lines on his graphs have recently been moving steadily downward. On 3,000 shares of Goodyear stock we have lost $16,801, on 800 shares of Eastman Kodak $3,882, on 1,800 shares of Memorex $22,347. Altogether our holdings are worth $50,-998 less than when Warner bought them for us. Reckoned another way, of course, the loss is even greater, for had we invested the money in some other way it would presumably have not just been holding its own but earning interest as well.

Not long ago I came across a newspaper article by the financial columnist Louis Rukeyser. He wrote, "This was the year when—for a change—just about everybody looked smart. It was hard, though not quite impossible, to recommend an investment that did not show a profit over the last twelve months."

I have finally had enough. I call Warner and tell him Alice and I have decided to try another way of handling our money.

Warner replies, "It's quite clear, I'm sorry to say, that you don't understand how the stock market works."

It seems to me, however, that I now know all too well how it works.

March 28

Alice and I ask a man we know at the Gruntal & Company brokerage house to put the money previously handled by Arthur Warner into municipal bonds. The ones he chooses are all top-rated for safety, and of course none are subject to federal taxes. It's hardly a daring investment policy, but it is something a financially unsophisticated mind like mine can understand. If, with municipal bonds, there is no hope of spectacular gains, there is at least little danger of enormous loss.

Only one regret troubles me. Two years ago in Los Angeles I went running in Griffith Park with a man named John Sporleder. Because Sporleder was a stockbroker, I asked him what he thought would be a sensible thing to do with some royalty income I was soon to receive.

"Put it into municipal bonds," Sporleder replied. "People who have money don't need to take risks."

It has taken me two years and a lost $50,000 to

come around to taking Sporleder's advice. Sometimes I am a slow learner.

Looking back over my conversations with the lawyer Arnold Zephyr and his colleagues, the investment advisor Arthur Warner, the spectacular manager Monty Casino and the other seers who have offered counsel, I see what my persistent mistake has been. I have clung to the innocent hope that I would find someone who, for a price, would live the bothersome parts of my life for me. The unhappy truth that this is an impossibility has finally seeped into my mind; like it or not, we each have to live our own lives. The other day a letter arrived from a man who identified himself as a senior financial planner for Shearson Hayden Stone. He advises me that unless I exercise caution, lawyers will dissipate my estate. I need Shearson Hayden Stone, he points out, to keep an eye on the lawyers.

Perhaps. But who would keep an eye on Shearson Hayden Stone?

March 31–April 16

An executive with WETA-TV in Washington, D.C., Jackson Frost, telephones. His station proposes to do a series called *Fixx on Foot*—"the kind of series," he writes in an eight-page description, "that PBS has been looking for for years." Frost has even prepared a budget: $694,059.

He and a WETA-TV fund-raising specialist, Sally Wells, fly to New York, rent a car, drive up to Connecticut, and take Alice and me to dinner at an expensive French restaurant. Bonhomie and optimism prevail. The only detail that remains, they say, is to find the appropriate underwriter to provide the necessary funds. With wine glasses we toast the project, whose start is clearly imminent. Thereafter Frost telephones me once or twice with progress reports, but our toast, it turns out, is in effect the end of the series, for nothing further happens. Presumably the Public Broadcasting System is still looking.

Television's mysterious silences and abysses are bewildering to an outsider. When a magazine editor gives an assignment to a writer, it is invariably genuine; the writer writes the piece, the editor usually accepts it, and the writer is paid the amount he has been told he would receive. In television, on the other hand, a baffling vagueness prevails. Vast enthusiasms are expressed and dizzying sums promised, but thereafter, much of the time, nothing happens.

At last I think I understand the difference. A magazine editor possesses, or has ready access to, money with which to pay the writers he hires. By contrast, a television producer—Matty Berrigan, Max Garfinkel, Jackson Frost or one of their multitudinous brethren—has only a smile, a shoeshine and an idea, either good or bad. When he is not actually producing a show, he is, for all practical purposes, penniless. Unless he is able to interest a sponsor, or in the case of public television a corporate benefactor, he has nothing. Hence, the reason you never hear from him again is that he is enormously busy doing something else. Having failed to find any enthusiasm for the program that involves you, he has moved on to another idea and another roster of potential backers.

Soon after *The Complete Book of Running* appeared, Julian Bach received an inquiry from a television producer who expressed an interest in buying rights to the book. I found the prospect exciting and was puzzled at what seemed to me Bach's casual indifference to the producer's interest. "You'll find,

Jim," Bach told me, "that television people are different from the people you meet in publishing." Now I
understand what he meant.*

At a party not long after the collapse of the WETA-
TV negotiations Alice has a conversation with Jean
Marsh, who is best known for her portrayal of the
servant Rose in *Upstairs, Downstairs.* Miss Marsh, a
writer as well as an actress, reports that she has recently been trying to interest Hollywood producers in
her television scripts. In doing so, she tells Alice, she
has noticed an odd and persistent phenomenon: agree-
ments repeatedly appear to have been firmly consum-
mated but then mysteriously fall apart. "I can't tell
you," she says, "how many times I've celebrated a sale
by going out and buying a new cashmere sweater. I
have a whole closet full of sweaters, but very few sales
to go with them."

April 18

A Pittsburgh runner writes in alarm, "I have encountered a problem that is not covered in your book. I am
being attacked by birds. This happens every spring in
Chicago when I visit my brother. They are red-winged
blackbirds, and their attack is real. This has instilled
such a fear in me that I'm told I turn chalk-white. I
apologize for bothering you, but with spring around
the corner I am truly desperate."

---

*When I finally do become involved in a television project, it happens
with surprising ease and dispatch. A Washington, D.C., company, R.B.V.
International, asks me whether I would be interested in making a videodisc
on the subject of running. A contract is drawn up, a $15,000 advance
against royalties and a $15,000 performance fee are paid, and in a few days
the show has been filmed. Subsequently RCA and MCA, among others,
offer it to the public in versions ranging from fifty-two to seventy-seven
minutes. Television, it seems, is like dynamite; it either goes off big or it
doesn't go off at all.

April 21

Bill Rodgers, one of the great marathon runners of all time, has written a book with the help of a *Boston Globe* sports staff member, Joe Concannon; it is published today, to coincide with the running of the Boston Marathon. (My own book, *Jim Fixx's Second Book of Running* appears today as well.) Called *Marathoning,* Rodgers's book describes his extraordinary running achievements and his thoughts about them and other aspects of the sport. Discussing books on the subject, he calls mine "the best all-around book on running."

Not every writer is so generous in his praise of rivals. Some, apparently fearing that a kind word for someone else's book may mean lost sales for themselves, go out of their way to denigrate the competition. One author, whose book appeared soon after mine did, claimed publicly that it was he who "taught Jim Fixx to run." In fact, I hardly knew him and had run with him only once or twice—a full decade after I had taken up the sport.

Rodgers is not only one of the most justly celebrated runners of his time but has also grown fairly wealthy as a result of his achievements. He operates a chain of sporting goods stores in and around Boston, makes frequent personal appearances, and commands large fees for whatever he does. Despite all the attention, he remains refreshingly unspoiled. He is one of the few top runners who, having raced twenty-six miles, will patiently linger until the last autograph seeker has gone home. It's no wonder he's as well liked as he is.

April 26–May 19

Thinking I might acquire a valuable autograph, I mail a copy of *The Complete Book of Running* to President

Carter. I receive only a perfunctory note from an aide.

Undaunted, I ask Cheryl Merser of Random House's publicity department to send the president a second copy. She does, but she, too, receives only a routine reply.

Finally I meet a woman, the mother of one of my son John's college classmates, who tells me she is deeply involved in the Carter reelection campaign. I describe my unsuccessful attempt to obtain an autograph.

"Send a copy of your book directly to me," she says. "I will personally deliver it to the White House. I guarantee you a letter from the President."

I mail her a copy, duly autographed. This time there is no acknowledgment at all.*

May 24

In Clearwater, Florida, I address a gathering of runners. Afterward one of them, a fit-looking man in his thirties, approaches me with a worried question.

"My training isn't going right," he says. "I'm just not getting the results I'm looking for."

"What kind of training are you doing?" I ask.

"It's easy to describe," he says, "since my workouts are exactly the same every day. At five-thirty in the morning I do a hundred situps and a hundred pushups. Then I run ten miles, fairly hard. At work I only get an hour for lunch, so the best I can do is fifty situps and fifty pushups and maybe a five-mile run. Finally, before bedtime, I do another hundred situps, another hundred pushups and then run seven or eight easy miles, just to relax."

---

*Months later I meet the presidential physician, Admiral William Lukash. He surprises me by saying, "The President loved your book. He was so enthusiastic that as soon as he finished it he passed it along to me to read."

I tell him that I'm afraid of going into oxygen debt just from listening to his recital. "It sounds as if you're getting in plenty of training," I say. "What's the problem?"

"I can't seem to develop any strength," he replies. "For some reason I'm always tired out."

June 14

I am in St. Louis, autographing copies of my new book in a department store. An attractive young woman asks me, "Are those by any chance your own legs on the jacket?"

I admit that they are.

"Will you marry me?" she asks.

July 6

My second running book has risen to No. 4 in the *New York Times.* It has been on the list for eleven weeks.

July 10

Giving a speech during the summer session of a university in Texas, I am billed, improbably in view of my usual fumbling, apprehensive style, as a "distinguished lecturer." (What, I wonder, is American higher education coming to?) And at North Carolina State University earlier this year, I was described as an authority who would help provide "a holistic glimpse into the future."

Apparently, what lies ahead has become a regular part of my beat. I have been asked to predict the future of sport in America, and for that matter the future of America itself. Irving Wallace and his son David Wallechinsky have even solicited my views for a successor to their *Book of Lists* called *The Book of Predictions.* (I have a lot of fun with this one. After all, the nice thing about long-range predictions is that almost no one goes back to compare what you foretold with what actually happens.)

Nor, in my preoccupation with the future that I am presumed to see with such luminous accuracy, have I been permitted to neglect the past. An editor at the *Washington Star* once telephoned to ask me to enumerate the best and worst occurrences of the past decade. "We're asking a lot of major thinkers," she told me.

"You came to the right place," I said.

July 21

A man writes from California: "I am an autograph collector. Recently a flood destroyed my entire collection. . . . "

August 13

A fifth-grade student named Paul writes from Newmarket, New Hampshire:

"I am making a survey of famous people I respect.

"My question to you is:

"Do you believe in God?

"If the answer is yes, please describe how God made his presence known to you."

September 21

Still clinging to the *Times* best-seller list. The book's twenty-second week!

October 12

In Washington, D.C., at a White House conference on sportsmedicine, I meet Joe Namath.

"Now that you've stopped playing football," I ask him, "do your knees still give you trouble?"

"All the time," he tells me. "Just standing here talking with you, I hurt."

Football, moreover, is not the only cause of his leg problems. "I was waterskiing," he goes on, "and I tore a hamstring muscle. The doctors tried to sew it together, but it's been so beaten up over the years that there was only so much they could do." He indicates his thigh. "Feel that," he says.

I put my hand on the hamstring. Beneath the skin, as big as a clenched fist, is a lump of mauled and mangled muscle. Namath, who is only thirty-six years old, has paid a heavy price for his renown. No matter what else may have happened to me, at least I don't hurt anywhere.

October 25

In the past several weeks I have given speeches in Boston, Washington, Charlotte, New York and Winter Park, Florida, and during the same period have appeared on quite a few television programs. It is only today that I have realized that it has not occurred to me to take tranquilizers in preparation for these appearances. Apparently while I haven't been paying attention, I have mysteriously cured myself of my longstanding phobia. *A.M. Chicago* seems a long time ago.

When I mention this to Alice, she reports to me a conversation she had recently with a friend who is a psychiatrist. She asked him, "Wouldn't many of the changes that occur as a result of psychotherapy take place anyway?"

"Certainly," the psychiatrist replied.

"Then why bother with psychotherapy?"

"Because," he said, "psychotherapy is faster than life."

Now that my anxiety has finally vanished, I see that I might perhaps have found a way to hasten its disappearance. Since the outcome has been satisfactory, however, I feel content with life's own pace.

November 12

A familiar voice on the telephone: "How's your supply of bee pollen?"

December 10

A letter arrives from an old friend and former boss, Harry Dahlheimer. He says, "I hope your success has earned you happiness as well as fame."

The sentence brings me up short. I now perceive a much slighter link between fame and happiness than I once did. If I am happier than I was before *The Complete Book of Running* was published, my happiness derives almost entirely from the new freedoms I find myself enjoying, and scarcely at all from the fact that I am better known and have more money. Increasingly, in fact, it seems to me that despite its considerable dazzle, being well-known is like a far-off fireworks display, which, although seen clearly enough, cannot be heard and thus offers the onlooker only part of its potential pleasure.

It sometimes seems, in fact, that friends and even strangers enjoy my well-knownness more than I do, and benefit from it in more obvious ways. A woman whom I quoted in *The Complete Book of Running* wrote me, "Thank you for giving me the little bit of celebrity I have," and several other people whose names I mentioned have told me of their amused delight at being asked for autographs. All this seems to me eloquent confirmation that the pleasures of renown glow more brightly the farther one gets from their source. (Or, as Susan Margolis aptly expresses it, "It happens more often than not that the real pleasures of fame exist more intensely in the minds of its observers, rather than in the private lives of the performer.")

This is the main reason I have nearly stopped putting any effort into my relationship with fame, and am now happy living in much the way I did before the book was published. Russell Baker once wrote about a celebrity who was "tired of being famous and is now satisfied simply with being rich." It seems to me he had something there.

A Sequel, and
a Speculation or Two

July 1981

Is it possible, I wonder, that I have been somewhat overconfident in my noisy insistence that success, for all its beguiling temptations, has altered me little? Several months have passed since the occurrence of the events described in this account. In culling the successive entries from journals, memoranda, letters, press clippings and memory and in shaping them for publication, I supposed—a trifle naively, it now seems to me—that my life was at last finding its way back to normal. As it turns out, this has not entirely been the case. For one thing, even in the now-you-see-it-now-you-don't hurly-burly of our times, success more often than not exerts a sustained rather than merely momentary undertow. Once you are in the public eye, you are likely to remain there longer than you expect. It is four years since *The Complete Book of Running* was published; by now, one might suppose I would have been largely forgotten. But no, in one recent week I was interviewed for most of an afternoon by a writer for a national magazine, held discussions with two sporting goods manufacturers who hoped, for a suitably persuasive price, to convince me that I ought to say some approving public words about their shoes and sweatsuits, devoted several hours to a television and radio project, and worked intermittently on this book and two short writing assignments.

It is not, however, merely such continuing busyness that leads me to suspect that I may have miscalculated the impact a best seller has on its author's life. Early in these pages, in comparing Marco Polo's experience with my own, I commented on—bragged about is perhaps more exact—how little I thought all the attention I had received had changed me. In the past several months, at least one circumstance has prompted me to wonder whether this is as true as I believed it to be. For Alice, who was so inextricable a part of this story, and I are now living apart from each other, and it seems unlikely that we will again dwell under the same roof. The reasons, so far as I am able to discover them, have little to do with the adulatory hoopla that was so suddenly and surprisingly called into being by my books. Still, the scarcely visible fault lines that ultimately shattered into tectonic fractures did, it is true, first begin to appear during the period covered by this account—after, that is to say, *The Complete Book of Running* became widely celebrated. It may be, therefore, that a clearer link exists between the two phenomena than I am clever enough to discern. It is, after all, a commonplace that where human relationships are concerned, fame is not infrequently an irritant. Just the other day I heard about a champion marathon runner whose name has been much in the news for half a decade and more; he and his wife, who had seemed exemplars of marital concord, are divorcing. A long list of similarly melancholy occurrences could easily be compiled.

Why such misfortunes so often bedevil those who are well known is not entirely clear. Is it that new wealth confers unfamiliar freedoms? Or is it perhaps that a celebrity, finding himself so generally admired, may be tempted to feel that he has thereby acquired a margin of grace and that, endowed now with a beneficence denied his fellows, he need no longer adhere quite so assiduously to the customary conventions and proprieties?

Both are probably true. On the other hand, I also suspect that relationships seldom crumble under the influence of fame, riches or anything else unless the fault lines, however microscopic or concealed, were already there.

About the Author

JAMES F. FIXX has been an editor of the *Saturday Review*, *McCall's* and *Life*. He has four children, and lives in Riverside, Connecticut. This is his sixth book.